A

MATTER

of

FACTS

A joint publication of the Society of American Archivists and the American Library Association.

ALA Neal-Schuman purchases fund advocacy, awareness, and accreditation programs for library professionals worldwide.

ARCHIVAL FUTURES

A MATTER *of* FACTS

The Value of Evidence in an Information Age

LAURA A. MILLAR

Foreword by Lee McIntyre

ALA Neal-Schuman | SAA

CHICAGO 2019

© 2019 by Laura A. Millar

Extensive effort has gone into ensuring the reliability of the information in this book; however, the publisher makes no warranty, express or implied, with respect to the material contained herein.

ISBN: 978-0-8389-1771-8 (paper)

Library of Congress Control Number: 2019943453

Book design by Kimberly Thornton in the Chaparral Pro and Brandon Grotesque typefaces.

♾ This paper meets the requirements of ANSI/NISO Z39.48-1992 (Permanence of Paper).

Printed in the United States of America
23 22 21 20 19   5 4 3 2 1

Contents

Series Introduction

"WHAT'S PAST IS PROLOGUE": IN *THE TEMPEST*, SHAKESPEARE REMINDS us that our actions up to this very moment provide context for our present decisions and actions. The accrual of this activity, in the form of the archival record, enables us to reflect on that past with tangible evidence in hand (or on screen). But recorded evidence doesn't just enable us to interrogate the present. We preserve the records and data of the present to provide evidence and context that will help us shape our collective future.

The Archival Futures series seeks to capture an irony that lies at the heart of the series title: Can what is past have a future, and vice versa? As a point of departure for critical thinking and for conversation, it centers the active role of archivists *and* all citizens in documenting society. Above all, it seeks to bring together all individuals who have a vested interest in cultural heritage and its stewardship, to both acknowledge and imagine the importance of the future archival record. This is a tall order.

When citizens find themselves without records and archives, memory, accountability, and transparency become precarious. We all share a collective, vested interest in the future of archives and must be partners in the preservation of the evidence of our present. Archivists act on behalf of the public good. Our work is focused outward and reflects the interests of many individuals and institutions. When archivists appraise records for enduring archival value, we imagine how people will use those materials; when archivists arrange and describe those records, we imagine how those descriptions might help people access important records; when archivists select technology and systems to serve as interfaces to our inventories and digital materials, we consider the ease with which people can find critical information; when archivists preserve and provide access to records, we imagine how those records will provide context for complex issues to society in the future; and when archivists consider the constellation of digital content on the Web—social media, hosted systems, local systems—and the fragility and ephemeral nature of that content, we understand our vital roles as stewards for the historical record, and our role in ensuring that these materials will exist in the future.

What makes this engagement of the archival record possible is a new approach to looking at the archival endeavor. By considering the work of archivists along with the theory that underpins that work, and by pairing that with ideas from contemporary trends in social theory, this series shows how the preservation and stewardship of the archival record is a collective effort that underpins and supports democratic societies and institutions. Our current times stand as a watershed for transparency, authenticity, accountability, and representation. These values are bound to the responsible preservation of our historical materials, and everyone should be concerned with the processes by which we accomplish this.

The decision to preserve a historical record is also undertaken in conjunction with allied professionals, such as librarians, museum curators, and information scientists, and is fundamentally future oriented. As the contributions to this series reveal, the notion of an *archival future* underlies all discussions concerning the responsibility to promote the preservation of records that document the full range of human activity. Archival practice necessarily responds to the past, the present, and the future. Archival professionals imagine a future—whether in the next century or a week from now—and strive to support the use of records in that future, by people not yet known, for reasons not yet imagined.

Through the contributions to this series, we want to open the discussion about the future of the archival record. We enter into this with the understanding that the archival record of the past informs contemporary society and that archival practice is a collaborative endeavor—between archivists, librarians, and citizens. Our stake in the future is written in the records and archives that represent us and tell our stories to future generations. What is past is not simply prologue; what is present is not simply epilogue; the records of the now are vital to the future of human society.

Bethany Anderson
Amy Cooper Cary

Foreword

EVER SINCE BOYHOOD, ONE OF MY FAVORITE THINGS TO READ HAS been dystopian fiction.

I'm not sure why it's always appealed to me. I don't like to read about space travel or weird life forms on other planets. But alternative views of what life on Earth might look like (what is sometimes called "social science fiction") have always captured my imagination. When I look back on the books that have really gripped me, I realize they were novels like George Orwell's *Nineteen Eighty-Four*, Aldous Huxley's *Brave New World*, Ray Bradbury's *Fahrenheit 451*, and in more recent years Margaret Atwood's modern classic *The Handmaid's Tale*.

Why these particular books? What is the attraction?

In addition to the horror of what happens to human beings in these novels, something that has always terrified me is the prospect of a world in which reality and truth are also under assault. Where human beings live in a world where they are made to feel crazy for wanting to float above the bullshit.

In *Nineteen Eighty-Four*, Winston Smith works in the Ministry of Truth as a censor. One day, when he finds incontrovertible proof that something has happened—which his government said did not happen—he holds it in his hands for a few seconds, before slipping it into the "memory hole" where it is lost forever. Orwell writes,

> [T]his was concrete evidence; it was a fragment of the abolished past, like a fossil bone which turns up in the wrong stratum and destroys a geological theory. It was enough to blow the Party to atoms, if in some way it could have been published to the world and its significance made known.

This is scary stuff. But then comes the really chilling part, which is when Winston asks himself the deeper philosophical question: What difference does it make whether such evidence once existed, if it does not still exist, and if the Party holds absolute power over present reality? Orwell continues,

> It was curious that the fact of having held it in his fingers seemed to him to make a difference even now, when the photograph itself, as well as the event it recorded, was only memory. Was the Party's hold upon the past less strong, he wondered, because a piece of evidence which existed no longer HAD ONCE existed? But today, supposing that it could be somehow resurrected from its ashes, the photograph might not even be evidence. . . . The past not only changed, but changed continuously. What most afflicted him with the sense of nightmare was that he had never clearly understood why the huge imposture was undertaken. The immediate advantages of falsifying the past were obvious, but the ultimate motive was mysterious.

The goal, of course, as Winston learns later in the book, is the achievement of power.

In *Brave New World*, books exist, but they are either suppressed or ignored. There are rumors of old forbidden books locked in a safe somewhere. But all books published before a certain date are prohibited. One character proudly proclaims that all of the books in libraries these days are books of reference, on the theory that if young people need a distraction they can get it at the "feelies." In *Brave New World*, entertainment comes from screens and sex and soma. A single copy of Shakespeare lies filthy and vermin-bitten, abandoned on the floor.

In *Fahrenheit 451*, the assault on evidence is even more overt, as books are burned as a means of controlling human behavior. In *The Handmaid's Tale*, women are not allowed to learn how to read.

Fast-forward to our present day, and we hear stories of the final days of the Obama administration, when people in the EPA and NASA were madly copying and disseminating documents to far-flung locations, guarding against the day when the Trump administration would come to power and perhaps decide to destroy the evidence about climate change. Even as I write this, the top news story on cable TV is one of censorship, where a political appointee of the president has full charge over redacting a 400-plus-page document that purports to tell the truth about whether a foreign power engaged in a cyber attack on our 2016 presidential election.

The control, fabrication, alteration, and destruction of evidence are no longer a thing of dystopian fiction. It is our present reality.

As Laura Millar writes in the preface to her quietly monumental book *A Matter of Facts*, it is her goal to stand up not just for facts but for evidence. What is the difference? For anyone who cares about truth, it is crucial.

In a digital age, the threat to reality is not just political but also technological. Imagine the tools of censorship in the hands of a 21st-century autocrat. In the past, authoritarian governments destroyed paper records (and sometimes the people who created them). Today, much of the evidence that serves as proof of historical and scientific facts exists only on computer servers and can be deleted at a keystroke. Orwell's question comes back to haunt us: If we cannot prove that something happened, did it really?

Ever since the 2016 election, there has been a push for archival protection under the threat of disappearance, against fading memory and political manipulation, of attacks on the truth-tellers in journalism and academics, even in law enforcement. Amy Siskind has been at the tip of the spear in guarding against this with her simply conceived book *The List*, in which she records—on paper—a list of changes made under the Trump administration, so that we will never forget what actually happened. In an interview, Siskind once commented on the reason that she finally relented and turned her digital blog into a physical book. At first she resisted but then one day realized that there was an advantage to having her list exist not just in virtual but also in paper form.

Must evidence be physical? No. But without a physical backup (and sometimes even with one), there is always the possibility of malfeasance. It is harder with a physical record. Electronic voting records can be compared to paper ballots. Digitally altered photographs can be compared to their originals. Text and audio can be scoured for evidence of manipulation.

The possibility of fakes will always exist, but without the presence of evidence, how will we know how to detect them? Millar has written a book of the utmost importance for those of us who care about the assault on facts, truth, evidence, and the values that uphold them. In this post-truth era, there are books aplenty that provide the historical context for what we are facing (Tim Snyder's *On Tyranny*), that trace out the lines of conceptual symmetry (Jason Stanley's *How Fascism Works*), and some that provide a philosophical defense of truth and evidence as well. But there are precious few that tell us what we can do right now to protect ourselves and our rights—other than voting and protesting—while we are living through this dangerous time.

Laura Millar's book does this, and brilliantly so. Though she demurs at one point and says that philosophy is "above my pay grade," I found much to learn from her careful dissection of the differences between data, information, evidence, facts, truth, and proof. But this is more than just a book of argument—or politics—for here we find fluid readable prose that tells a compelling story.

A Matter of Facts is (unfortunately) not a work of fiction; the threat of dystopian reality has now migrated from the world of make-believe to the one we actually inhabit. But never fear because you now hold in your hands one of the texts that will help you to make sense of this world. Like Orwell and Bradbury, like Stanley and Siskind, Laura Millar has written a book that people in the future will look back on and say, "This is one of the books that helped us to survive until a new era."

Lee McIntyre
April 2019

Preface

I AM A DIGITAL IMMIGRANT. WHEN I WAS A CHILD, THE ONLY TELEPHONE in our home was a black rotary dial model that sat on the hall table. By the time I was a teenager, we had a second phone. It had a cord long enough that I could sit on the staircase and imagine I was having a private conversation with my best friend, even though my mother always seemed to have something essential to do just within earshot. When I bought my first personal computer in 1984, the machine, keyboard, 10 megabyte hard drive, and dot matrix printer (along with an ink cartridge and a pack of bond paper) cost me over $5,000. Today, I cannot escape technology. My husband and I own two desktop computers, four laptops, three iPhones, three iPads, and a digital photograph album. We are living, breathing examples of the transition society is making from analog to digital.

I have worked as a recordkeeping consultant for nearly 35 years. I have helped governments establish policies to manage digital evidence, and I have rescued boxes of deteriorating paper files from flooded basements. I have consulted with national and state governments in Canada, the United States, Fiji, Sri Lanka, Trinidad, Hong Kong, and Zambia. I have sorted archival photographs with retired volunteers in local historical societies, helped First Nations governments in the Canadian Arctic preserve oral histories and traditional stories, and provided advice on electronic records management to international agencies like the United Nations. Through my career, my recordkeeping goals have been the same: to protect trustworthy sources of evidence so that agencies remain accountable; people's rights are protected; organizations can uphold their responsibilities; and communities have access to the documentary touchstones that allow them to shape identities and share memories.

I have written this book because I see a crisis before us. An evidence crisis. I want to convince you that evidence—which is different from data, information, or facts—is critical to accountability, identity, and memory, and ultimately to democracy. If we are going to survive these perilous times for the world—and they are perilous—we need evidence. We need access to government reports that demonstrate whether public officials are fulfilling their promises; to property documents that prove we own our land; to birth certificates that verify our citizenship or trace our lineage; and to archival photographs that help us recollect past times. Because so many of these sources of evidence are now digital, we cannot just assume they are going to survive as trustworthy sources of proof. We all must look differently at how we capture, preserve, share, and protect our sources of evidence. Otherwise we may not be able to access these critical sources of proof when we need them.

I have written this book for the public, not for my professional colleagues. I draw on news events rather than scholarly treatises. I tell stories rather than analyze theories. I am taking a risk here, of course: writing for my peers has become a (relatively) comfortable place to be. Explaining contemporary recordkeeping issues to the public, on the other hand, is a tricky business, especially in today's fraught and fast-moving political climate, when the news keeps changing day by day. The stories I recount here will probably have changed by the time this book is in print; new sources of evidence will challenge existing interpretations. But that's the whole point of evidence. The more we have, the better our understanding. Which is why we need evidence so badly. And the more we have, the better our ability to assess the truth. Evidence-based truth, not personal truth.

In this book, I am calling on you, the public, to join us, the recordkeepers, to become the "we" in "we must work together to protect evidence in the digital age." So even though I sometimes refer to my own professional group of recordkeepers as "we" and "us," more often I am referring to all of us: you, me, our families, our workmates, our fellow colleagues, or our classmates. Everyone. We need to come together to create a new movement. An evidence movement. We need a call to arms for the protection of authentic evidence. I hope that by the time you finish this book you will join me in this quest for change. We can and must work together to protect evidence as a trustworthy foundation of a just and democratic society.

Introduction

A wise man, therefore, proportions his belief to the evidence.
David Hume, 1777

THE CAREER TRAJECTORY OF ARCHIVISTS LIKE ME, WHO STARTED IN
a predigital world, is not what we expected. After receiving my graduate degree
in archival studies in 1984, my first job was to help a local historical society
organize its archival photographs and old diaries. I worked out of the basement of a local school and spent a lot of my day drinking tea and listening to
the volunteers, all in their seventies and eighties, reminisce about the adven-
tures of their teenage years. Some three decades later, I spend my days writing
electronic records management and digital privacy policies; advising on the
costs, risks, and benefits of digitization as a tool for preservation and access;
and recommending procedures for separating important email communications from the thousands of duplicates cluttering corporate records systems.

When I say I am trained as an archivist, though, many people look puzzled.
Either they don't know what an archivist is, or they assume I am a librarian or
historian. I am not a librarian; I can't develop a collections policy or catalog a
book. I am not a historian, though like all archivists I am quite competent at
historical research—it's a fundamental part of the job. Some people think that
I trace family trees for a living, like the researchers on *Who Do You Think You
Are?*, or that I appraise artifacts, like the experts on *Antiques Roadshow*. No and
no. At the furthest edges of misunderstanding, some people see me as a real-
life Indiana Jones and assume that I go on expeditions to find lost treasures. I
consider archives treasures, but I don't crawl through snake-infested jungles to
find them. (Heaven forbid.) One devotee of Stieg Larsson's thriller *The Girl with
the Dragon Tattoo* compared me with the cyberpunk computer hacker Lisbeth

Salander. That confusion was quickly corrected. I am decades older and entirely tattoo free.

Yes, archivists work with historical resources and publications and databases. We preserve photographs so that the village can create displays for its 100th anniversary. We photocopy newspaper clippings so that the local historian can find references to the Great Flood of 1948. We digitize old documents so that undergraduates can study the Stock Market Crash of 1929. We develop digital recordkeeping systems so that government officials can find contracts and correspondence quickly. We are trained to find logic and order in a pile of boxes or a cluttered shared drive. Creating order out of chaos is one of our great strengths.

But we are not "just" archivists. We *are* archivists. We are recordkeeping professionals; evidence keepers; protectors of proof. Our goal is to preserve documentary evidence not only for a group of people but for all of society, however that society is defined: nation-state, geopolitical community, indigenous culture, ethnic group, whatever.

Back in the day, we might have been called monks or scribes, curators or collectors. Today we might be called records managers, information officers, business process analysts, risk assessment specialists, access and privacy officers, or compliance managers. Our titles don't matter. What matters is that we keep evidence so that people can access and use that evidence however they want—whether to build a connection with their ancestors, prove their right to a pension, achieve justice in a court of law, or find documentary proof of a precious but vague memory from their childhood. The evidence we preserve and make available might be used in a legal case, as part of an anniversary celebration, in treaty negotiations, or as an illustration in a Ken Burns–style documentary film. And once one person has used the evidence we protect, the recordkeeper returns it to safe custody, as authentic and trustworthy proof, so that the next person can use it, for whatever purpose. Our goal is to preserve a trail of accountability, whether the trail is made of stone or paper, cellulose film or computer chips. We protect trustworthy evidence so that it may be used for any purpose, from the defense of rights to the identification of responsibilities, from the protection of identities to the sharing of memories or the telling of stories.

Recordkeepers are guided in this work by our ethical codes, which demand that we act as responsible stewards of evidence, defending its authenticity and integrity. We have an obligation to be as impartial and objective as possible. Our job is to protect the most authentic evidence, not just the evidence we like, in the same way a judge must uphold the law, not just the laws she likes, and a journalist must respect the facts, not just the facts he prefers. Sure, we have opinions, ideas, and perspectives, like everyone else. But our primary responsibility is to serve as witness. Ever since hooded monks crept out of the castle with manuscripts under their tunics, to keep precious evidence from being destroyed, we have done all we can to ensure that trustworthy sources of proof are preserved, so that they can stand as *proof.*

In an information age, though, recordkeepers cannot do this work alone. We cannot wait for evidence to become "old" before we protect it. We cannot wait for records to pass slowly from office to storage room to archives over the course of a century. Digital sources of proof may not survive a year, never mind a century, if we do not protect them from harm from the moment they are created.

As I discuss in chapter 1, in the post-truth world we live in today, we are drowning in data, inundated by billions and billions of sources of information and evidence, from digital photographs to emails to text messages. At the same time, we live in a world where truth is a vanishing species; where lies and deception are becoming all too common and too easily accepted. To counter the onslaught, we—we the public, not just we the recordkeepers—need to understand the difference between truth, facts, and evidence, as I consider in chapter 2. Of course, we all carry personal truths. No one can deny me my right to believe that pancakes come from heaven. But some truths must be based on evidence: on sources of proof outside our own memories. But as I examine in chapter 3, what distinguishes evidence from data and information is its quality as a trustworthy and verifiable source of proof, ideally authentic, complete, and unchanged. And as I outline in chapter 4, evidence can take many forms, from a clay tablet to a digital photograph. The photographs of a Civil War battlefield are evidence, even though the photographer may have taken some liberties to make the image more evocative. A piece of data in a database can also serve as evidence, but only if we know why and how it was put in the database in the first place. Pieces of wood can be evidence, and so can Twitter messages. The complexity of modern evidence makes its management so much more complex today than it was three decades or three centuries ago.

But why should we care about evidence anyway? What is it good for? As I consider in chapter 5, records, archives, and other documentary sources help us confirm who we are and how we fit in the universe. They are tools we use to shape our identities and make connections. Evidence is also crucial to support justice and protect rights, as I suggest in chapter 6. How can we fight against war crimes without documentary evidence of atrocities? How can we ensure that refugees are protected without trustworthy proof of their rights and entitlements? And as I discuss in chapter 7, evidence also helps us craft personal and collective memories or adjust false or inexact recollections. Records and archives are the stuff of history, but historians are not the only ones who rely on evidence for their work; journalists, authors, and scientists turn to sources of evidence to enhance their analyses and shape their narratives.

But evidence, particularly digital evidence, can be manipulated. As I illustrate in chapter 8, statisticians can misrepresent facts and ignore documentary proof in their quest to assert the findings they want. Leakers and whistleblowers may feel they are doing a service by releasing evidence to the public, but if they are not careful, the evidence they distribute could make conditions worse, not better. Computer hackers expose us to the dark side of evidence by hijacking, stealing, or destroying essential sources of proof. How can a society function if governments and businesses are locked out of computer systems or documentary evidence is held hostage?

If we are going to counter these threats and ensure that trustworthy sources of evidence remain accessible as tools to support accountability, foster identity, and preserve memories, we need to act. First, we need to shed some of our assumptions about evidence, as I discuss in chapter 9. We should not assume that our evidence laws are adequate or that our privacy is guaranteed. We should not accept that evidence is safe or that technology is stable. And we should not continue to march into a digital future without thinking hard— much harder than we do now—about the implications of digital technologies, not only for evidence but also in terms of economics, democracy, equality, and environmental sustainability.

Once we have readjusted our perspective on evidence, we need to act. As I argue in chapter 10, we need to acknowledge that evidence is not a casual by-product that can be overlooked on the assumption that it is okay and will remain so in perpetuity. On the contrary, evidence is a crucial resource that needs to be managed from the moment it is created, and for as long as it is needed, even if that is forever. We need to provide this enduring care by strengthening laws, improving the effectiveness (not just the efficiency) of technology, and raising public awareness of the importance of protecting trustworthy evidence. We need to work together, actively and persistently, to protect our society's documentary sources so that they can serve as evidentiary links between our past, present, and future. And we need to use these sources of proof actively and enthusiastically, as tools that allow us to tell stories, share memories, connect with our communities, or seek out the traces of our personal or collective past.

In the end, if we do not protect evidence, we cannot protect evidence-based truth. We will end up losing our trust in the instruments of democracy, as evidence is replaced with opinion, as good laws are overcome by bad, and as the rule of law is flouted by people in power whose priorities are not the same as the public they are supposed to serve.

We need to act. But *we* are not just recordkeepers. *We* are not just politicians or bureaucrats or lawyers, statisticians or journalists. *We* means everyone. Today, each one of us probably accumulates as much evidence in a year, or a week, as our grandparents did in their lifetimes, and we store it all on a cell phone in our pocket. Given the fragility of digital technologies, we need to act vigorously and decisively if we are going to ensure that trustworthy evidence continues to serve as a protection against lies and deceit.

The time has come to change course. We need to find a new and more effective way—a collective and cooperative way—to combat lies. Evidence helps us support human rights, fight for justice, create a sense of identity, and shore up precarious memories. Evidence is the antidote to the toxicity of a post-truth, post-fact world. More than that, the diverse sources of evidence we create every day—records, archives, photographs, diaries, letters, text messages, tweets—serve as touchstones. They show the world that we were here. That we mattered. Without evidence, we all become just rumors and whispers and shadows. I hope you will join me in the fight for truth—for evidence-based truth.

1

"Fake news" and "Truthiness"

The Value of Evidence in a Post-Truth World

I have faith in the people. They will not consent to disunion. The danger is, they are misled. Let them know the truth, and the country is safe.
Abraham Lincoln, 1861

IN AUGUST 1977, *NEW YORK TIMES* JOURNALIST LEE DEMBART reported on the Computermania exposition in Boston. He interviewed exhibitors and enthusiasts to understand why anyone would want to own the latest innovation on display: the personal computer. One sales representative likened computers to automobiles: people didn't see the value of a car in 1850, but now cars are indispensable. One day soon, he argued, computers would be seen the same way. Manuel Ulloa, a student at the Massachusetts Institute of Technology, offered the rather cryptic suggestion that he would want a personal computer because "you can take it in your room and turn the lights out." (To each his own.) Steve Jobs, who had cofounded Apple Computer only a year before, suggested that financial investors could use his $1,300 Apple II computer to chart stock prices, and radio operators could use it to figure out frequency skips. (Again, to each his own.) But Jobs admitted that "most people are buying computers not to do something practical but to find out about computers." Dembart left the show stumped. "No one could say for sure why people might need a computer at home," he concluded. "'For fun' seemed the most honest answer."[1]

In today's information age, we use digital technologies for everything from the practical to the whimsical, the legal to the criminal. According to the statistics and business intelligence portal Statista, only 8.2 percent of Americans had a computer at home in 1984. By 2015, nearly 90 percent of Americans owned a personal computer. By 2018, however, most owners of personal computers were over 30 years old. Fewer than 50 percent of people 18 to 29 years old owned a personal computer. More than 95 percent of them owned a smartphone instead.[2]

We are surrounded by technology. Using that technology, we create more evidence now than we ever have before, but that evidence does not sit in static paper documents, the way it did only a few years ago. We don't write letters like we used to; instead we send text messages and post status updates to Facebook. We don't log financial transactions in bound ledgers; we input data into electronic spreadsheets. More and more of us pay our bills online, not with checks, and we share photographs on Flickr or Instagram rather than print pictures and mail them to each other. Even if we end up with a physical object in our hands—a printed report, perhaps, or a framed photograph—that object almost inevitably began life as a collection of bits and bytes.

Drowning in Data

One of the computers on display at the Computermania show in 1977, the IMSAI microcomputer, came with a hard drive that provided 10 megabytes (MB) of digital storage.[3] (A byte is a unit of digital memory consisting of eight smaller units called bits.) That 10 megabytes, or 10 million bytes, may have seemed a cavernous digital space when a single floppy disk held 160 kilobytes. But a 10 MB drive will hold only one two-minute YouTube video, and not a high-definition studio production but a simple "How do you do it?" or "Look at my cute cat" video. Today people post over 300 hours of video to YouTube every minute. Can you imagine how many 10 MB hard drives we would need to store 300 hours of cat videos? (Okay, since you asked: 1.2 million.)

According to technology expert Bernard Marr, people around the world generate 16 million text messages, 156 million emails, and 1 trillion photographs every day.[4] This adds up to 2.5 quintillion bytes of data whirling across the globe. *Every day.* One quintillion is one with eighteen zeros after it. That number is unfathomable to me, but then I shudder at the sight of a decimal point. I have, with great effort (and a lot of help from clever friends), calculated this: if 2.5 quintillion bytes a day is equivalent to 2.5 billion gigabytes a day, then we generate 912.5 billion gigabytes of data every year. Now, the Hubble telescope (which despite its declining age still provides us with such amazing images of faraway galaxies) streams back to Earth about 17.5 gigabytes of raw data a week or 910 gigabytes a year. If we wanted to transmit all the data we generated in a year—912.5 billion gigabytes—from the Hubble telescope back to Earth, it would take . . . wait for it . . . one billion years. One million millennia. *Ten million centuries.*

Sure, we have faster technologies now than the Hubble telescope. But that's not the point. We also have faster, more powerful cars. A lot of good that has done us: our cities and countries are now designed around a dependence on combustion-engine vehicles, just when we seem to have realized that perhaps we ought to have developed more sustainable, less damaging transportation technologies in the first place. We are drowning in digital "stuff" and the only answer cannot be to design bigger life jackets. When scholars talk about the digital paradigm shift—the transformation from the mechanical and analog world to the digital world—part of what they are talking about is the reality that societies are generating such unfathomable volumes of information. But volume is not our only challenge. The real difficulty is determining what is valuable as evidence, why, and for how long.

It is easy to argue that property records or legal contracts are valuable evidence; how would we prove our rights without them? And we can feel confident that shopping lists or restaurant reservations are not worth keeping for very long; world affairs will likely not change if I cannot prove I purchased bananas last week. But what about family photographs? Are they all valuable? Only some? Which ones? What about government reports? Which ones are important? On which topics? Why? What about cat videos? Are they valuable? Which ones? Siamese cat videos get kept but tabby cat videos get tossed?

Some of the documentary content we create in a day is useful evidence for just a moment. Other items are critically important for decades, centuries, or millennia. But sources of evidence are valuable only if we can trust them. We need to know that our property records can act as legitimate proof that we own our house and garden. We need to know that our birth certificates are authentic, so that we can prove our legal identity and maintain a sense of connection with our family and ancestors. We need to know that our family photographs paint an accurate picture of our lives: how can we be honest about our family's past if Uncle Joe, the black sheep, has been cut out of the picture?

Back when evidence came in paper form, such as documents, reports, or printed photographs, or in analog form, such as sound recordings or celluloid films, we could confirm authenticity much more easily. It was easy to see if a letter was missing pages, a photograph had been cropped, or a report had been edited. It was not hard to see the splices in a film or hear the skips in an audio-cassette. It is much harder to see changes in digital evidence. How do we know that Uncle Joe has been cut out, or that Uncle Joe even existed? How do we know that a government pronouncement is authentic if it comes in the form of a tweet—posted on Monday, deleted on Tuesday, and reposted with completely different wording on Wednesday?

Our ability to trust digital sources of proof is seriously compromised by the very technology that we have incorporated so deeply into our lives. It is extremely hard to verify the authenticity of evidence that sits in a black box on our desk, in a server farm in another city, or in the mysterious cloud (which is, in fact, just someone else's computer). We can't see the stuff. How can we trust it?

Living in a Post-Truth Age

In the second decade of the 21st century, digital technologies are ubiquitous. Is it a coincidence that, at the same time, many of us are becoming so distrustful? As we embrace digital technologies, it is becoming harder and harder to distinguish something authentic from something fake. Is this why fewer and fewer of us trust official pronouncements of facts, whether from government officials, journalists, or corporate leaders? Or is there some other reason many of us trust feelings over facts?

"Post-truth," Oxford Dictionaries' word of the year in 2016, was defined as "relating to or denoting circumstances in which objective facts are less influential in shaping public opinion than appeals to emotion and personal belief." The comedian Stephen Colbert called it "truthiness." We can feel in our heart that something is true. Does it really matter if the facts suggest otherwise?[5]

I am not a philosopher. I am an archivist. Philosophy is well above my pay grade. But with apologies to philosophers from Plato to Bertrand Russell, I think we have got ourselves a serious case of what I call the postmodern blues. We live in an age when many people think it is reasonable to reject science, research, and reason in favor of suggestion, interpretation, and nuance. They argue that there is no authentic or objective truth. That our differences are just as important as our similarities. That artistic creations such as novels, paintings, musical compositions, or architectural designs are merely subjective constructions. That we all bring our own sensibilities to making or interpreting anything. That everything comes with a bias.[6]

The academic arguments around the postmodernist approach, which became popular in the mid-20th century, are fascinating. I don't think it is unreasonable to agree that we all bring our own perspectives to everything we see and experience. I might read a novel, see a film, or view a sculpture and carry away a different interpretation from the next person. Fair enough. But we have taken a step beyond postmodernism now. We have gone from a time when we recognized the existence of bias to a time when we seem to reject the existence of objective truth. Some people see bias not just in artistic creations but in documentary evidence, dismissing government reports as lies, scientific studies as opinions, and media reports as "fake news." Have we gone too far? Where is the truth if there is no truth?

There are many types of truth. We have the right to our own personal truths. We are entitled to believe, or not believe, that God exists, or that women have the right to an abortion, or that cats are better than dogs. For some of us, those truths are irrefutable; for others, they are debatable. Facts will not help us prove the "truth" of any of them. But facts are essential to proving, for instance, that wearing a seatbelt is safer than not, that smoking cigarettes can cause cancer, or that dropping out of high school limits employment opportunities for young adults. But we can prove the truth of these statements only if we have access to facts. And those facts should be based on verifiable evidence: statistical analyses of car accidents; medical research into tobacco and cancer; sociological studies of the relationship between education and employment. The challenge is knowing whether we can trust the evidence.

I fear that our society is slipping into a dangerous post-truth sinkhole, where truth and trust are drowning in the flood of conflicting data and opinions. If people keep sliding down this hole, soon there will be less and less respect for the law and for the rule of law. Laws, after all, are built on facts and evidence, and the rule of law is based on the idea that no one person is above the law.

What happens to democracy then? Democracy is underpinned by a society's acceptance of the law, the rule of law, and the legitimacy of facts and evidence. If people give up on evidence-based truth in favor of personal truth, we are all bound to collide with each other, aren't we? And what comes of that? Factionalism; tribalism; extremism. Conflict. Chaos.

We may be in a "postmodern" age or a "post-truth" age. Are we also in a post-fact, post-trust age? As we lose our trust in facts, we seem to be losing our faith in humanity, culture, and democracy. What an ideal environment for demagogues and autocrats to sweep in and take power. As the philosopher Lee McIntyre has argued, "What is striking about the idea of post-truth is not just that truth is being challenged, but that it is being challenged as a mechanism for asserting political dominance."[7] Hannah Arendt, the philosopher who saw firsthand the handiwork of Adolf Hitler and the Nazis during World War II, wrote that "the ideal subject of totalitarian rule is not the convinced Nazi or the convinced Communist, but people for whom the distinction between fact and fiction (i.e., the reality of experience) and the distinction between true and false (i.e., the standards of thought) no longer exist."[8]

As we churn in this storm of bits and bytes, the lifeline hanging before us has been tossed out by power-hungry brigands who promise us that they are the only ones telling the truth, all the while working overtime to hide any evidence that proves otherwise. Is there a connection between the digital deluge and this vortex that is the post-truth age? If so, how can we pull ourselves out?

Valuing Evidence

Evidence is the real lifeline. We cannot respect the law, or the rule of law, if we do not respect and demand trustworthy evidence from governments, corporations, the media, other decision makers, and each other. We cannot defend human rights, foster a just society, support identity, and nurture memory if we do not capture, protect, and share evidence of life outside our own small personal worlds. We ignore evidence at our peril.

But what is evidence, really? Why is it different from information? It's all just data, isn't it? No, it's not all "just" data. As I discuss later, data are some combination of elements of raw content, such as numbers or letters, sounds or smells. Information is contextualized data, infused with layers of meaning. Evidence is any source of information that provides demonstrable proof. Your fingerprint provides forensic proof of your identity. Your DNA provides scientific proof of your genetic makeup. Your birth certificate provides documentary proof of your existence on Planet Earth. The type of evidence I focus on in this book is recorded evidence: information that can be fixed in space and time and verified as authentic. Documents, photographs, tweets, data in a database. Authentic original sources, not excerpts or interpretations. Verifiable proof.

As I hope to demonstrate, only a small portion of recorded evidence has enduring value. Archives are the small documentary portion of all the evidence we create in our lives and work that we choose to keep forever, for our own benefit and for the benefit of society. As the South African archival scholar Verne Harris has argued, societies only retain a "sliver of a sliver" of all the documentation they produce.[9] For centuries, the identification and preservation of this precious core of documentary evidence have been the specialty of the archivist: the evidence keeper. But in a digital environment, recordkeeping professionals cannot wait for governments, businesses, or families to create sources of documentary evidence, *then* wait for those sources to be put away safely, *then* wait for them to grow old, *then* collect the small portion with enduring value, and *then* identify it, organize it, and preserve it so that it may be used by society for as long as possible. This traditional, linear process worked reasonably well in the days of paper records and metal filing cabinets. It does not work in today's digital world.

There is no guarantee that digital evidence will last long enough to make it into a storage repository. Computer technologies make it frighteningly easy to manipulate data, whether intentionally or by accident. People create, edit, duplicate, and delete electronic records all the time. How much vital evidence is stored on an unlabeled USB key tossed in the back of our desk drawer? How many digital duplicates of duplicates of duplicates do we have in a project folder on our computer? How often have we found ourselves halfway through a business negotiation only to realize we are working with the wrong electronic record? I know I am not alone in these experiences. I make my living helping people overcome them.

Learning by Example

Guaranteeing that our digital evidence is safe, authentic, and complete—that it is trustworthy—demands that we change our understanding of data, information, and evidence. Completely. All of us who create records and evidence need to remember that not everything we create is "just" data. Some sources of evidence have immeasurable long-term value. But if we mix up the enduring with the obsolete, we end up either keeping everything, which leaves us drowning in data, or losing too much, which sinks us further into a post-truth, post-fact, post-trust mire.

To help us change course, we can learn from the example, both good and bad, of society's efforts to protect our environment. Some people, like Rachel Carson, sounded the alarm early on. She warned us of the "silent spring" that would come if we persisted in using pesticides and poisons on our land. But many of us did not listen. How many people still struggle to accept that global warming is now scientifically undeniable?

We have not done all we could to reduce the threat to our environment, but we have made a bit of progress, in some parts of the world. We have, at least, raised awareness of the problem, though we are a long way from achieving sustainable solutions. We have established laws that help to reduce pollution and improve environmental care; whether they are followed adequately is another question. We have replaced wasteful and energy-draining technologies with more efficient tools, even though we haven't addressed the huge costs associated with the transition. And we have heightened public awareness of the importance of protecting our planet, though too often those in power do not seem to listen. Still, we are slowly learning to follow the dictum *Reduce, Reuse, Recycle.* We are starting to change our thinking about the environment. I think we are realizing, albeit slowly, that we cannot take it for granted that Planet Earth will always be there for us.

What if we made similar improvements in the management of evidence? We could strengthen laws to require that good evidence is created, kept, and made available, and that unwanted information is destroyed by policy, not personal whim. We could build more effective computer technologies to lock down digital evidence, so it cannot be changed or deleted without permission, while filtering out superseded materials more efficiently. We could teach everyone from business executives to schoolchildren the value of evidence, so that they can distinguish between proof and conjecture, facts and lies. Such changes are possible. And they are necessary.

In an age when information can be manipulated so easily, the very essence of democracy is threatened when people can no longer rely on—or even find—impartial and objective evidence. As we sink into the morass of data and evidence, we are increasingly at the mercy of gangsters masquerading as populists and snake oil salesmen pretending to be saviors. It isn't just the risk of bias; bias is nothing new. It's always been there; we just only lately started to recognize it. But these days we are in danger of more than fake news and twists in interpretation. We are seeing the loss of evidence, by accident and by design, as people manipulate sources of proof in their effort to blur the lines between reality and fantasy. We need to draw together all our resources to put a stop to the lies. One of those resources is evidence.

I care passionately about the protection of evidence. I believe that a life worth living is a life of integrity and honesty. I see evidence as a bulwark against attacks on that integrity and honesty. Trustworthy records and reliable data give us a factual foundation that allows us to distinguish between truth and lies. Truth matters. Facts matter. Evidence matters more.

NOTES

1. Quotes are from Lee Dembart, "Computer Show's Message: 'Be the First on Your Block,'" *The New York Times*, August 26, 1977, www.nytimes.com/1977/08/26/archives/computer-shows-message-be-the-first-on-your-block.html *archived at* https://perma.cc/83DX-3HJ6.

2. See the data from Statista, "Percentage of Households in the United States with a Computer at Home from 1984 to 2015," https://www.statista.com/statistics/214641/household-adoption-rate-of-computer-in-the-us-since-1997, *archived at* https://perma.cc/VK5H-TU84; "Share of People That Own a PC/Mac Stationary or Desktop in the United States in 2018, by Age," https://www.statista.com/statistics/368406/individual-computer-ownership-usa, *archived at* https://perma.cc/2P3V-3BG5; and "Share of Americans Using a Personal Cell Phone [. . .] in 2018, by Age,"

https://www.statista.com/statistics/231612/number-of-cell-phone-users-usa, *archived at* https://perma.cc/J29T-DDHV.

3. See IMSAI, "IMSAI Announces Hard Disk" (press release, 1978), https://classictech .files.wordpress.com/2010/03/1978-imsai-announces-hard-disk-cdc-hawk-9427h .pdf, *archived at* https://perma.cc/B26C-KESY.

4. See Bernard Marr, "How Much Data Do We Create Every Day? The Mind-Blowing Stats Everyone Should Read," *Forbes*, May 21, 2018, https://www.forbes.com/sites/ bernardmarr/2018/05/21/how-much-data-do-we-create-every-day-the-mind -blowing-stats-everyone-should-read/#3c38b31a60ba, *archived at* https://perma .cc/Q3WU-DHFN.

5. See OxfordDictionaries.com, "Word of the Year 2016 Is . . . ," https://en.oxford dictionaries.com/word-of-the-year/word-of-the-year-2016, *archived at* https:// perma.cc/4RBY-QU6C. For Stephen Colbert's take on Oxford's choice, see Jethro Nededog, "Stephen Colbert Takes Credit for the 'Post-Truth' Era We're Living In," *Business Insider*, November 18, 2016, http://www.businessinsider.com/stephen -colbert-post-truth-oxford-word-of-the-year-2016-11, *archived at* https://perma .cc/Y37V-7VAD.

6. The literature on postmodernism is deep and dense. A good starting point is Brian McHale, *The Cambridge Introduction to Postmodernism* (London: Cambridge University Press, 2015). Another overview can be found in C. Stephen Evans, *A History of Western Philosophy: From the Pre-Socratics to Postmodernism* (Downers Grove, IL: IVP Academic, 2018). In the 1990s, many archivists embraced Jacques Derrida's *Archive Fever: A Freudian Impression*, trans. Eric Prenowitz (Chicago: University of Chicago Press, 1996), as a call to incorporate postmodern philosophies into the world of recordkeeping and archives management.

7. Lee McIntyre, *Post-Truth* (Cambridge, MA: MIT Press, 2018), xiv.

8. Hannah Arendt, *The Origins of Totalitarianism* (New York: Harcourt, Brace, Jovanovich, 1976), 474.

9. Verne Harris, "The Archival Sliver: Power, Memory, and Archives in South Africa," *Archival Science* 2, no. 1 (2002): 63–86.

2

"Rarely pure and never simple"
Truth, Facts, and Evidence

Two plus two is four. Three plus one is four.
Partly cloudy, partly sunny. Glass half full, glass half empty.
Those are alternative facts.
Kellyanne Conway, 2017

ON JANUARY 20, 2017, DONALD TRUMP WAS INAUGURATED AS THE 45th President of the United States. The next day, at his first briefing as White House Press Secretary, Sean Spicer rebuffed media reports that the crowds were smaller than for previous inauguration ceremonies. Spicer argued that "this was the largest audience ever to witness an inauguration—period—both in person and around the globe." He substantiated his point by providing a series of facts: the area closest to the platform where the president was sworn in holds about 250,000 people; the next area some 220,000 people; and the next 250,000. According to Spicer, 420,000 people used the DC Metro transit system that day, over 100,000 more than for Obama's 2013 inauguration. All these facts, he said, proved how large the crowd had been. The media, he complained, had misstated the crowd size.[1]

As well, Spicer argued, the media had intentionally framed photographs of the proceedings to minimize the "enormous support" shown for President Trump. The manipulation of information was a "shameful" attempt to "lessen the enthusiasm of the inauguration."[2] The next day, senior White House aide Kellyanne Conway defended Spicer. Rejecting NBC journalist Chuck Todd's argument that Spicer's statements were "a provable falsehood," Conway argued that the media had presented one set of facts and Spicer had offered a set of "alternative facts."[3]

Did Spicer tell the truth? Or did he present us with alternative facts? What are the facts? What is the truth?

Linking Truth to Evidence

As Oscar Wilde said, the truth is "rarely pure and never simple." Whole libraries are devoted to treatises on truth. Philosophers have invented correspondence, coherence, and constructivist theories of truth, as well as consensus and pragmatic theories and the morose-sounding deflationary theory. Scholarly debates about truth have persisted for millennia, and the arguments are growing to a fever pitch in this post-truth age. Metaphysical discussions about the meaning of truth are beyond me, I confess. My concern with truth, in this book at least, is not whether beauty is truth or vice versa. My interest is in how truth relates to facts and how facts relate to evidence. But we need to define truth if we are even going to start the conversation.

The word *truth* derives from the Old English *trȳwe* or *true*, meaning "steadfast or loyal." Not infallible or unchangeable, and not fact-based or provable. Steadfast. Loyal. Faithful. *True.* Truth can be objective or subjective, definitive or conditional, whole or partial. There is no one unassailable personal truth. A Catholic may accept as true that Jesus is Lord. A mother may accept as true that she knows exactly why her baby is crying. A conspiracy theorist may accept as true that the 1969 Apollo moon landings were fabricated on a Hollywood movie set. I accept as true that Bugs Bunny cartoons are the zenith of animation. It would take an overwhelming supply of contradictory evidence to shake these personal truths. Even then some people will never be persuaded otherwise.

Other truths depend heavily on facts. I tell the truth when I say it is raining at my house if and only if raindrops are falling, consistently, outside my door. We tell the truth when we say the earth rotates around the sun because we have ample proof of the fact, from telescopic observations to astronomical data to visual images from space. (Thank you, Hubble.) Galileo Galilei was not so lucky. Absent the weight of evidence available today, Galileo was convicted of heresy when he challenged accepted thought about the structure of the universe.

We tell an evidence-based truth when we say that the human immunodeficiency virus (HIV) is transmitted between humans through the exchange of fluids such as blood, semen, vaginal liquids, or breast milk. Scientific facts back up this truth. But South African President Thabo Mbeki rejected those facts, arguing in the late 1990s that the people suffering from a mysterious ailment were afflicted not by a transmissible virus but by poverty and poor nutrition. Choosing personal truth over documented proof, Mbeki rebuffed offers of international funding and medical aid. It has been argued that more than 300,000 South Africans died of AIDS-related illnesses as a direct result of personal truth masquerading as policy.[4]

People are entitled to their own opinions. But as American Senator Daniel Moynihan said decades ago, people are not entitled to their own facts. The only way to ensure that evidence-based truths are substantiated is to ensure we have access not just to the facts but to the evidence that validates those facts.[5]

What do I mean, then, when I talk of truth, facts, and evidence? I define an evidence-based truth as a conclusion or perspective reached as a result of the analysis of an accumulation of facts. A fact is a statement that is consistent with reality or that can be proven by an analysis of available evidence. Evidence is any source of information that provides demonstrable proof. Evidence may take many forms: physical, scientific, legal, forensic, and so on. My interest here is in recorded evidence: information that has been fixed in space and time and can be verified as authentic, so that it serves as proof.

We link truth with evidence in different ways. We can test some truths by comparing our assertions with reality: we see rain falling from the sky and confirm it is raining outside. The puddle forming on our front drive, the physical evidence of falling rain, helps to substantiate our assessment. We use scientific evidence such as astronomical observations to confirm the earth rotates around the sun. Medical analyses provide scientific evidence that HIV/AIDS is caused by a virus. But to prove or disprove other types of truth, we rely not on assertions of reality or on physical or scientific evidence but on recorded evidence: documentary proof.

Comparing Truth and Evidence

Imagine that one sunny Sunday afternoon a man is gunned down on the street. How can we determine the truth about who committed the crime? Police officers and lawyers might look for physical and scientific evidence. Does forensic analysis prove that *this* bullet was fired from *that* gun? Are there fingerprints on the gun? Are the prints the same as the suspect's? Are there witnesses, and are they reliable? Perhaps two men saw the suspect fire the gun and tackled him immediately. They can provide direct evidence about the event, brave fellows. The link between evidence, fact, and truth is airtight.

But what if we have no bullet, no gun, and no suspect-tackling eyewitnesses? Perhaps, several hours after the shooting, Mr. Kantor saw a suspicious-looking person a block away from the crime scene. Mr. Kantor is convinced he saw the man responsible, but he did not see the actual crime in progress. Mr. Kantor's witness testimony may add to the case for or against the suspect, but the strength of his statement depends on the reliability of both his memory and his eyesight. The link between evidence, fact, and truth might be tenuous.

Personal observation is not a consistent source of indisputable truth. A climate change denier may argue that because 25 feet of snow fell in her backyard last winter, there is no global warming. Certainly, the snow in her yard is a fact. But the research conducted by the National Aeronautical and Space Administration (NASA) and the Intergovernmental Panel on Climate Change, based on the study of long-range climate data, examination of ice cores, review of satellite imagery, and statistical analysis of weather patterns, provides unequivocal scientific evidence of climate change. The snowfall is a fact. But the evidence of snow in one person's backyard is a weaker form of proof than is evidence drawn from extensive, scientifically rigorous climate research.[6]

Accommodating New Evidence

Of course, facts can change as new evidence is discovered. When I was a child, there were nine planets in the solar system. My favorite was Pluto. Who wouldn't love a planet named after a dog? (I was never much for Greek mythology. I prefer cartoons.) But in 2006, Pluto suffered an ignominious demotion, going from planet to dwarf planet. As astronomers invented new tools, they discovered more potential planets in the region of the Kuiper Belt, including Quaoar (identified in 2002), Sedna (2003), and Eris (2005). Each of these celestial bodies was as large as or larger than Pluto. How, the astronomers asked, could Pluto be a planet while those other bodies were not?

To address this definitional challenge, the International Astronomical Union established a committee to define the characteristics of a "real" planet. They developed mathematical models and used them to gather and assess scientific evidence. In the end, Pluto (and Quaoar, Sedna, and Eris) fell short of the mark. We went from nine planets to eight. (I was heartbroken. All I had left was the dog.) But in 2016, astronomers theorized there was another planet, about 10 times the mass of Earth. So how many planets are there? Eight? Nine? Ten? If astronomers keep creating larger and more powerful tools to gather new evidence, the "true" number of planets will keep changing. New tools, new evidence, new truths.[7]

In 1666, Isaac Newton put forth a theory that there was such a thing as gravity. (Whether he was struck on the head by an apple remains a debatable point, but it's a great story.) Newton posited his theory and brought together a series of facts, including extensive scientific data. He ended with an evidence-based truth: masses attract each other, and the gravitational force between two bodies is proportional to the product of their masses, while inversely proportional to the square of the distance between them. I don't understand the theory, but I know that apples fall to the ground. I accept as truth that Newton's explanation is correct.

Or I used to. In 1915, Albert Einstein came up with a new theory. Like Newton, Einstein tested his theory by bringing together a series of facts and evidence. But Einstein had a lot more resources at his disposal. Scientific and mathematical tools had improved mightily over the centuries. In the end, Einstein came up with a new truth. Gravity is not static; it becomes stronger or weaker depending on differences in space and time. I don't understand Newton's theory, and I *really* don't understand Einstein's theory. But I accept that a lot of scientific evidence lies behind E = MC².

Putting Truth in Perspective

Sometimes the truth of an answer is directly proportional to the assumptions behind it. Is Mount Everest the tallest mountain on earth? Yes, *if* we measure mountains from sea level to the summit. The summit of Mount Everest reaches 8,848 meters above sea level. But if we measure differently, then, no, Mount Everest is not the tallest mountain on earth. If we measure from the ocean floor instead of from sea level, then Mauna Kea in Hawaii, at 10,200 meters, is the tallest mountain on earth, even though only 4,205 meters of Mauna Kea are above the sea. So, which is the tallest mountain on earth? We face the same relative truth with the name itself: Mount Everest is known as Sagarmāthā in Nepali and Chomolungma in Tibetan. Which is the "true" name? The answer changes as soon as we adjust our assumptions about language and culture.

Degrees of truth exist in our daily lives too. A yogurt manufacturer may tell the truth when it says its yogurt contains no fat. But one serving of a fat-free "diet" yogurt might contain the equivalent of five teaspoons of sugar, making it less nutritious than a serving of ice cream. Does "fat-free" equal "healthy"? Or is the yogurt manufacturer banking on the shopper's assumptions to make a sale? A wise consumer does not accept marketing slogans but reads nutrition labels.

A fellow may tell the truth when he says he has been married only once. Sure, he has participated in only one formal, legally binding marriage ceremony. But he may have lived in five common-law relationships before his one legal marriage. His perception of "marriage" may conform to religious or civil laws, but the sixth person invited to move in with him may want to unpack some assumptions about the definition of marriage before unpacking the pajamas and toothbrush.

Recognizing Truth as a Social Construct

Some truths are not based on fact at all; they are the result of shared understanding. We may all accept as true that a Euro is worth 100 cents. But, a five Euro note is simply a piece of paper with ink on it. Because a fiat currency like a Euro is not backed by a commodity, such as gold, silver, or jewels, it has no intrinsic value. Its relative value is entirely dependent on government policies, stock markets, and trade agreements. Given the ongoing, angst-filled political drama associated with the anticipated departure of the United Kingdom from the European Union (a decision now deferred until October 2019), and the consequent threat to the stability and cohesion of the European Union, there is no guarantee that the Euro will exist a quarter century from now.

Another social construct is the division of the planet into geopolitical entities. For instance, it is true that there is a border between the United States and Canada. In fact, both Americans and Canadians like to boast that we share the longest undefended border in the world. But there is no immovable line on the ground providing evidence of the division. Proof that the border exists is found only in recorded evidence such as treaties and legal agreements. There is no obligation to maintain the border as it is; it has been interpreted and reinterpreted many times since the days of the American Revolution. The border persists today only through mutual goodwill and a shared belief that a promise is a promise.

The Euro is only a quarter century old. There is no guarantee it will remain. The Canadian-American border was not always there. There is no guarantee it will remain. Further, currencies and national borders do not exist for birds or deer or bears or wolves or fish, and they can be highly contested symbols for indigenous people. Social constructs such as currencies and borders are true only if all parties agree that they are true. If not, well, that way lie referenda, lawsuits, and wars.

Distinguishing Truths from Lies

Sometimes people just don't tell the truth. One might suggest Donald Trump is perhaps the best-known liar in politics today. He has been caught telling lies about everything from election results to meetings with Russian officials to the number and nature of his relationships with women. To find some piece of evidence-based truth in Trump's statements, whole armies of journalists and fact-checkers rake through documentary sources. Since Trump took office in January 2017, *The Washington Post* has been tracking the number and nature of his false and misleading claims in a regular column called "The Fact Checker"; the journalists have estimated that in the first nine months of his presidency, Trump made 1,318 false or misleading claims, an average of five a day, but that in the seven weeks leading up to the midterm elections on November 6, 2018, his daily quota of lies rose dramatically, reaching some 30 false or misleading claims every day. As of April 2019, the tally had risen to 9,451.[8]

Some say that all politicians lie as naturally as they breathe. When I was in elementary school, though, my teachers held up George Washington as the golden exception: he *never* lied. Guess what. He did. In June 1780, during the American Revolution, Washington colluded with Major General Lafayette, his French ally, to write a proclamation declaring that the French army was going to help the revolutionaries free Canada from the British. Washington wanted to take New York City, and he figured that if he could deflect British attention to the Canadian border, he would have a clear path. To mount the deception, Washington drafted the fake proclamation and sent it to the military commander in Philadelphia to be printed.

Washington's expectation was that the printer would leak the news to the British. What Washington didn't realize was that the military commander at the time, Major General Benedict Arnold, was a first-rate British spy. The news was leaked, but history is silent about whether the leak came from Arnold or the printer. Regardless, the British were deceived, and Washington was able to proceed with his plans for the Canadian border. Many Americans, then and now, might consider this fake proclamation an acceptable lie. (My husband, who happens to be Benedict Arnold's great-great-great-great-grandson, is an exception. He thinks the story shows how duplicitous Washington could be. The cherry tree business? Lies, lies, and more lies.[9])

Other lies are useful only to the person lying. In 1998, Bill Clinton claimed, under oath, that he "did not have sexual relations with that woman," the White House intern Monica Lewinsky. But his assertion was rebutted by facts and evidence. Lewinsky saved the gifts Clinton gave her and did not clean a dress she wore during one of their sexual encounters, thus preserving both physical and forensic evidence. As well, Lewinsky's conversations with her friend Linda Tripp about the affair were recorded. This physical, forensic, and documentary evidence proved that Clinton and Lewinsky were engaged in an intimate relationship. This evidence gave substance to other accusations of impropriety, leading Congress to start impeachment proceedings against the president. Clinton was eventually acquitted of the charges of perjury and obstruction of justice, but no one can deny he offered an extremely narrow "truth" about the relationship, based on an Old Testament interpretation of "sexual relations."[10]

Moving from Truth to Proof

To argue that the crowd at Trump's inauguration was the largest ever, Spicer defined how many people could stand in the space surrounding the inauguration platform and how many people rode the subway that day. It might be possible to substantiate those statements with a bit of forensic research. We could count the number of chairs set out on the platform, or we could calculate the number of people who could stand in one spot on the National Mall and multiply by the space available. We could review transit data to find out how many people rode the subway to the inauguration site instead of to some other place in the city. But statements about potential capacity do not tell us how many people *were* there, only how many people *could* have been there. Such is the power of the conditional tense.

The other way to verify the statements, if we were Dr. Who and had access to a TARDIS, would be to travel back in time and hold the inauguration over again. Then we could install turnstiles at every entry point to the National Mall, controlling the process of ingress and egress. We could issue tickets, so we would know exactly how many people entered the space. We could take photographs of everyone as they entered the Mall and use facial recognition software to confirm that people were not counted twice. These are all reliable methods for accurately documenting large crowds of people. But we haven't mastered the art of time travel, so we can't go back and start again. More importantly, most democracies—at least those with respect for the rule of law, privacy, and individual rights—frown on such zealous methods of crowd control.

All we can really do is rely on the recorded evidence generated at or immediately after the event: photographs and video recordings, eyewitness accounts, and newspaper reports. We can use that evidence to provide a reasonable estimate of the size of the crowd. As it turns out, there is an abundance of recorded evidence available, including news footage, cell phone recordings, aerial photographs, and social media messages. By analyzing all this documentary evidence, we can come up with a more accurate estimate and equate that evidence with comparable sources for previous inauguration ceremonies. Only then can we determine with a fair degree of certainty if the 2017 inauguration was, in fact, "the largest ever."

Journalists and researchers have done just that: combing through sources of evidence to look for verifiable proof. In a report on January 21, 2017, Reuters News Agency confirmed that the two photographs it presented to show the differences in crowd size between 2017 and 2009 were taken from the same location on the top of the Washington Monument. One was taken at 12:01

p.m. on January 20, 2017, and one sometime between 12:07 and 12:26 p.m. on January 20, 2009.[11] The two images serve as authentic proof of the size of the crowd at comparable times on each inauguration day.

The New York Times, Getty Images, and *PBS NewsHour* produced photographs and time-lapse videos showing that the 2017 crowd did not stretch as far as Spicer claimed. Steve Doig, a professor of journalism at Arizona State University who had assessed crowd size for the 2009 inauguration, examined satellite imagery of the 2017 event, concluding that Obama's crowd was "three times larger."[12] Keith Still, a professor of crowd science at Manchester Metropolitan University in the United Kingdom, estimated that the crowds at Trump's inauguration were about one-third the size of those at Obama's 2009 inauguration and only two-thirds the size of those at Obama's 2013 ceremony.[13] Data from the Washington Metropolitan Area Transit Authority's Vital Signs Report for January–March 2017 show that the combined use of trains, buses, and other transit services for January 2017 was 24,226,632, two million *lower* than the forecast of 26,272,000.[14]

Of course, before we can accept the validity of these external sources of evidence, we need to verify their authenticity. Spicer suggested (didn't he?) that the media might have manipulated evidence in order to deceive. In the digital age, this is a legitimate concern. We should not just accept evidence without ensuring it is authentic, complete, and unchanged. Are the photographs date stamped? Is there any sign that images or video recordings were altered? Can we confirm the accuracy of the numbers in the transit reports? Were the forecasts objective and reliable? Were the statistical analyses based on sound methodology?

As it turns out, researchers did assess the authenticity of evidence, filing access to information requests with the US government for official records related to the inauguration. They discovered that records used to assess crowd size had been manipulated. Aha! Spicer was right! In September 2018, the UK newspaper *The Guardian* reported that it had received evidence, gleaned through responses to access requests, that a photographer *had* edited official photographs of Donald Trump's inauguration to make the crowd appear larger than it was. Not a newspaper photographer. A government photographer. The photographs had apparently been edited "following a personal intervention from the president." The response to the access requests also pointed to Sean Spicer as having been "closely involved in the effort to obtain more favourable photographs."[15]

It certainly does sound like someone did arrange to reframe photographs "intentionally," with deception in mind. That someone, it appears, worked for the White House. New evidence. New facts. New truths.

By itself, the "My inauguration is bigger than your inauguration" battle seems like an insignificant issue: a question of ego, not policy. But the continued debate about something so unimportant, especially when the facts are staring us in the face, highlights a more serious disease. We live in an age when too many people prefer feelings over facts. It is too easy to reject verifiable evidence and provable facts in the search for alternative facts and personal truths. And it is far too easy for unscrupulous agents to capitalize on this weakness in our collective consciousness for their own personal benefit. Stephen Colbert's concept of "truthiness" captures today's zeitgeist all too well. We can feel something to be true, even if it is not. So, who cares if it is not?

I believe we should care. It has become far too easy to manipulate data, alter information, and render evidence unreliable. We all have the right to hold on to our personal truths. I have every right to believe that Elmer Fudd singing "Kill the Wabbit!" to the tune of Wagner's "Ride of the Valkyries" is sublime. My husband has every right to enjoy his familial association with Benedict Arnold, as long as he tones down the rhetoric when visiting the American side of the family. But it is not right that hundreds of thousands of people might die of a disease like AIDS because someone in power refuses to accept scientific and medical evidence. It is true that $2 + 2 = 4$ and $3 + 1 = 4$. These are alternative ways of calculating a sum. But they are not alternative facts. There is only one true 4, whether it is counted as $1 + 1 + 1 + 1$ or $2 + 2$ or $3 + 1$ or $4 + 0$. 4 exists.

Facts exist. We need to respect them. When societies disrespect verifiable facts and trustworthy evidence, we are in grave danger of imprisoning truth-tellers for heresy. If truth is a conclusion or perspective reached as a result of the analysis of an accumulation of facts, and if a fact is a statement that can be proven by an analysis of available evidence, *and* if evidence is any source of information that provides demonstrable proof, then in order to defend truth and reject lies, we don't need facts alone. We need evidence.

NOTES

1. See White House, "Statement by Press Secretary Sean Spicer," January 21, 2017, https://www.whitehouse.gov/briefings-statements/statement-press-secretary-sean-spicer, *archived at* https://perma.cc/8GG9-DAB2.

2. Ibid.

3. "Conway: Press Secretary Gave Alternative Facts," interview by Chuck Todd, NBC's *Meet the Press*, January 22, 2017, https://www.nbcnews.com/meet-the-press/video/conway-press-secretary-gave-alternative-facts-860142147643, *archived at* https://perma.cc/2ULE-TCLU.

4. See Lee McIntyre, *Post-Truth* (Cambridge, MA: MIT Press, 2018), esp. chapter 1. See also Sarah Boseley, "Mbeki Aids Denial 'Caused 300,000 Deaths,'" *The Guardian*, November 26, 2008, https://www.theguardian.com/world/2008/nov/26/aids -south-africa, *archived at* https://perma.cc/7W6P-4M76.

5. Moynihan's quote has become so popular it is difficult to hunt down the original source; readers might prefer to study his thinking by reading his own collection of letters, *Daniel Patrick Moynihan: A Portrait in Letters of an American Visionary*, ed. Steven Weisman (New York: Public Affairs, 2010).

6. NASA publishes many of its reports online at https://climate.nasa.gov/evidence, *archived at* https://perma.cc/N4Q7-9JNG, and the Intergovernmental Panel on Climate Change does the same at http://www.ipcc.ch/report/ar5/wg1, *archived at* https://perma.cc/RQ8V-3Z22.

7. Samuel Arbesman discusses the changing interpretation of Pluto as a planet in his fascinating book on how scientific facts change over time, *The Half-Life of Facts: Why Everything We Know Has an Expiration Date* (New York: Current, 2013).

8. See Glenn Kessler, Salvador Rizzo, and Meg Kelly, "President Trump Has Made 6,420 False or Misleading Claims over 649 Days," *The Washington Post*, November 2, 2018, https://www.washingtonpost.com/politics/2018/11/02/president-trump -has-made-false-or-misleading-claims-over-days/?utm_term=.c3222f08deb0, *archived at* https://perma.cc/X4B2-9WET, and Kessler, Rizzo, and Kelly, "President Trump Has Made 9,451 False or Misleading Claims over 801 Days," *The Washington Post*, April 1, 2019, https://www.washingtonpost.com/politics/2019/04/01/ president-trump-has-made-false-or-misleading-claims-over-days/?utm_term =.8b289117ccd2, *archived at* https://perma.cc/5JYE-FX8Y.

9. The correspondence outlining Washington's plan can be seen on the Library of Congress website at https://www.loc.gov/resource/mgw4.066_0511_0513/?sp=1, *archived at* https://perma.cc/2ERX-M567. The letter to Benedict Arnold including the proclamation can be seen at https://www.loc.gov/resource/mgw4.066_1047 _1048/?sp=1, *archived at* https://perma.cc/WQ56-YW87. See also The Washington Project website at the University of Virginia, which includes transcriptions and summaries of historical documents, http://gwpapers.virginia.edu, *archived at* https://perma.cc/7QJQ-BPYN. A discussion of Washington's proclamation is pro- vided in Benjamin L. Huggins, "George Washington Tells a Lie," The Washington Papers, January 22, 2016, http://gwpapers.virginia.edu/george-washington-tells -a-lie, *archived at* https://perma.cc/22RH-7PUD.

10. A comprehensive analysis of the Clinton-Lewinsky story is Marvin Kalb's *One Scandalous Story: Clinton, Lewinsky, and Thirteen Days That Tarnished American Journalism* (New York: Free Press, 2001).

11. See Jeff Mason and Roberta Rampton, "White House Accuses Media of Playing Down Inauguration Crowds," Reuters.com, "Politics," January 21, 2017, https:// www.reuters.com/article/us-usa-trump-media-idUSKBN15600I, *archived at* https://perma.cc/9NUZ-HL8R.

12. See Lori Robertson and Robert Farley, "The Facts on Crowd Size," Factcheck.org, *The Wire*, January 23, 2017, https://www.factcheck.org/2017/01/the-facts-on -crowd-size, *archived at* https://perma.cc/S3YA-Z9LX.

13. See Sarah Frostenson, "A Crowd Scientist Says Trump's Inauguration Attendance Was Pretty Average," *Vox*, January 24, 2017, https://www.vox.com/policy-and-politics/ 2017/1/24/14354036/crowds-presidential-inaugurations-trump-average, *archived at* https://perma.cc/YQ3A-KERD.

14. Washington Metropolitan Area Transit Authority, *Vital Signs Report—Q1/2017* (May 2017), https://www.wmata.com/about/records/scorecard/upload/Vital _Signs_Report_Q1_2017_Final1.pdf, *archived at* https://perma.cc/WZ4M-M8ZY.

15. Jon Swaine, "Trump Inauguration Crowd Photos Were Edited After He Intervened," *The Guardian*, September 6, 2018, https://www.theguardian.com/world/2018/ sep/06/donald-trump-inauguration-crowd-size-photos-edited, *archived at* https:// perma.cc/SXU2-NGZP.

3

"Given under my hand"

The Nature of Evidence

*A multitude of particular facts cannot be seen separately,
without at last discovering the common tie which connects them.*

Alex de Tocqueville, 1840

WHEN BARACK OBAMA RAN FOR PRESIDENT OF THE UNITED STATES
in 2007, rumors circulated that he had not actually been born in Hawaii, as
he claimed, but in Kenya, East Africa. Article 2, section 1, of the United States
Constitution forbids anyone from being elected president if that person is not a
"natural born citizen."[1] If Obama had been born in Kenya, he could not be president. So, on this matter, Obama's word was not good enough. The dissenters
demanded proof.

To satisfy them, Obama released a copy of his short-form birth certificate
in June 2008, showing that he was born in Hawaii, at 7:24 p.m. on August 4,
1961. But that was not good enough for some. Even after Obama won the election, controversy swirled. In 2011 the White House released a copy of Obama's
long-form birth certificate, showing he was born Barack Hussein Obama II on
August 4, 1961, at Kapiolani Maternity & Gynecological Hospital, 6085 Kala-
nianole Highway, Honolulu, Hawaii. The document also identified his father,
Barack Hussein Obama, age 25, born in Kenya, East Africa, and his mother,
Stanley Ann Dunham, age 18, born in Wichita, Kansas.

What made this second document more believable than the first? And what
made both documents more trustworthy than Obama's word? The long-form
certificate, with its green paper, black type, and multiple boxes holding discrete
bits of data, carries an aura of authenticity. It is signed by doctors and regis-
trars, stamped with dates, and certified as true. It is seen as more reliable than
Obama's word alone.[2]

The path from fact—Obama is born—to evidence—Obama was born on August 4, 1961, in Honolulu, Hawaii—is not always straightforward. If we are going to understand the nature of recorded evidence as a trustworthy form of documentary proof, we need to start by understanding the difference between data, information, and evidence. Then we need to know what makes evidence trustworthy and what happens when that trustworthiness is not guaranteed.

Moving from Data to Evidence

We are bombarded by data from the moment we wake up, and the torrent continues throughout the day. In the morning, as I lie in bed, I hear birds singing, see the glow of sunrise, and feel the weight of the duvet. When I tuck in at night, I hear the rain outside, feel my husband toss around in his sleep, and smell the scent of the fresh sheets. This is all data. Data, from the Latin *datum* or "(thing) given," is one or more elements of raw content, such as images, smells, letters, numbers, or symbols. Information, on the other hand, is contextualized data, layered with additional meaning. My knowledge and experience tell me that two data elements, birdsong and raindrops, are different. I hear the sounds, analyze the data, and generate information.

After we receive data and convert it into information, we might decide to communicate it to someone else. I might hear sounds outside, convert the data to information, and exclaim to my husband that the birdsong is lovely this morning. Or I might hear the raindrops, convert the data to information, and ask my husband to close the window to keep the room dry.

Sometimes it takes more than personal knowledge and experience to analyze data and convert it into information. 8,848 is a data element. 420,000 is a data element. 8 is a data element. But these data elements could mean anything. To understand them, we need more context. As it happens, 8,848 is the height, in meters, of Mount Everest; 420,000 is the number of people who rode the Washington, DC, subway system on January 20, 2017; and 8 is the number of planets in the solar system. (This week—who knows what the astronomers are plotting next.)

Much of what we say and do in a day goes along entirely undocumented, coming and going like birds on the wind. This is, I believe, a Good Thing. An unexamined life may not be worth living, but second-by-second documentation of our daily existence is a serious case of Too Much Information. (A perspective perhaps not shared by the people who post Instagram photographs of everything from the bruise on their toe to the fried eggs they cooked this morning.) But still, we might choose to capture information, like a bird in a net, so that it exists in a fixed form. Maybe we need to ask someone for help and can't ask them in person. Maybe we want to remember something special and share it with our friends. Maybe we want to document a controversial experience, so we have proof in case we are questioned later.

When I send my husband a text message asking him to buy milk on the way home, I have generated a communication and initiated an action. I ask for milk; he acquires milk. (All marriages should operate this seamlessly.) But the process of extracting that information from my brain and capturing it in external form does more than result in a communication or an action. It also creates a potential source of evidence.

There is a great benefit to extracting information from our brains and capturing it in an external form. First, we no longer need to hold the information in our heads. We have transferred it to a fixed medium, such as a Post-it note, report, photograph, clay tablet, parchment scroll, or tweet. This transfer of information frees our minds to consider the next piece of information that comes our way. I don't have to remember asking my husband to buy milk because I have created an external reminder.

As well, by lifting the information out of our head and turning it into an external, static object, we can share that documentary evidence more easily. Other people can use the evidence—the record—even if we are not around. My husband does not need me in the room to know he needs to buy milk. He has the text message in his phone. This makes life much easier, not only for marriages but also for bureaucracies. If ten, fifty, or a thousand people are going to work together successfully, they need to leave information and evidence for each other, so everyone can carry on with their own work independently.

Finally, by creating a static, external source of evidence, we have an authentic form of proof. If my husband claims I did not ask him to buy milk, I can show him the outgoing text message in my phone and say, "Yes I did." The existence of that information gives me the (small) joy of knowing I was right. We all rely on photocopies of reports, copies of emails we sent, or the text messages in our phones as proof of our "side" of actions, transactions, and communications.

The word *record* derives from the Latin recordari: re for restore and cor (from cordis) for heart. A record "restores by heart." Records help us to do something, document something, and remember something. Records also help us prove something, serving as evidence of what we did, said, or thought. That evidence can be used tomorrow or a century from now, if we protect it so that it remains authentic and usable.

Having fresh milk might be vitally important when I want a cup of tea, but history will not change if future generations do not have documentary evidence of my family's shopping habits. Other types of evidence hold much more value. One example is the 2018 report of the Information Commissioner's Office (ICO), which investigated the use of data analytics in political campaigns in the United Kingdom.[3] Another is the 2019 US Department of Justice (DOJ) report, by Special Counsel Robert S. Mueller III, which looked into allegations of Russian interference in the US election in 2016.[4]

In the UK example, the allegation that prompted the ICO investigation was that, in the lead-up to the 2016 "Brexit" referendum on whether the United Kingdom should remain in the European Union, a political consulting firm called Cambridge Analytica accessed and used personal data from nearly 90 million Facebook users around the world without their knowledge or permission.[5] The ICO investigated charges that Cambridge Analytica extracted or "scraped" (what a dreadful word) data from Facebook pages including, for instance, personal name, birth date, city of residence, and whether someone "liked" a page on Facebook. Cambridge Analytica was then accused of using this information to target individuals with political campaign advertising during the referendum. The results of the referendum were painfully close: 48.11 percent voted to stay in the European Union and 51.89 percent voted to leave. In its investigation, the ICO found that Cambridge Analytica and other agencies had carried out not only negligent behavior but outright contraventions of the law, including multiple breaches of regulations around privacy and data protection. Those responsible, the ICO argued, showed a "disturbing disregard" for personal privacy.[6]

The American investigation, which began in May 2017, examined allegations of Russian interference in the 2016 US presidential election: the first question was whether there had been any conspiracy between US government officials and Russian operatives; the second was whether the president or other officials obstructed justice by interfering in the investigation. Despite the president's protestations that there was "no collusion, no obstruction," Mueller found extensive evidence of "sweeping and systematic" Russian interference in American electoral processes, and he identified numerous links between individuals associated with the Russian government and individuals associated with the Trump campaign. Mueller did not, however, secure enough evidence to meet the high standard required for criminal charges; as he noted, the investigators faced significant challenges in the search for verifiable evidence. As Mueller concluded,

> If we had confidence after a thorough investigation of the facts that the President clearly did not commit obstruction of justice, we would so state.

Based on the facts and the applicable legal standards, we are unable to reach that judgment. Accordingly, while this report does not conclude that the President committed a crime, it also does not exonerate him.[7]

The ICO and Mueller reports both serve as useful examples of the concepts I explore here. They are both official records, which provide authentic evidence of actions, transactions, or decisions. But they are not the only source of authentic proof of the cases they examine. Correspondence, witness statements, interview transcripts, press releases, social media posts, and other records generated throughout these investigations provide additional documentary evidence. All these sources are essential now, to provide governments and the public with verifiable facts about what happened. The sources will still be useful decades and centuries from now, to provide accurate proof of the events surrounding Brexit, Facebook, Cambridge Analytica, Russian espionage, American elections, Donald Trump's presidency, and who knows what other topics.

To remain trustworthy sources of evidence, the reports and the associated records need to be protected. There is no iron-clad guarantee they will remain authentic and reliable proof unless they are secured, from the moment they are created, as evidence. We need to be able to guarantee that they were created according to agreed rules and norms, preserved with their authenticity intact, and made available in keeping with the dual responsibilities of access and privacy.[8]

Protecting sources of recorded evidence against accidental loss or malicious attack is increasingly difficult. When paper records were filed in a central storage repository, under lock and key, their security, while not guaranteed, was more certain. Documents might be removed from offices according to an established schedule, kept in a storage facility for several years so that staff could access them easily, then moved into an archival facility (a government repository in the case of the official UK or US records), and then made available for the government and the public to use. Today, even with the best of intentions, an agency such as the ICO or the DOJ could be attacked through cyberspace: digital documents could be revised minutes after they were created; whole files could be deleted from computer systems; and statistical data sets could be manipulated to replace actual findings with false results.

Digital records are at risk because of the combination of velocity, volume, and veracity. Electronic evidence moves with lightning speed. It is not easy to capture an official record before it is deleted, by accident or design. Nor is it easy to find the official record among a hundred different versions of a document. Protecting a report, email, photograph, database, or other source of evidence so that it is authentic, complete, and trustworthy is challenging at the best of times, but dramatically more so in the information age.

Defining Data, Information, and Evidence

I will spend much of the rest of the book discussing the value of evidence. But I must start with some core definitions. As I have already considered, *data* are some combination of elements of raw content, such as numbers or letters, and *information* is contextualized data, or data infused with layers of meaning. A *record* captures information or data in a fixed medium; it is a "whole" thing: an email, a report, or a text message. *Evidence* is any source of information that provides demonstrable proof. We cannot say that a Facebook post is only information, or a photograph is always evidence, or a database is just data. If the source—data element, photograph album, or membership database—can be used to provide proof of actions, transactions, or decisions, then it has evidential value.

Just because something has value as evidence, though, doesn't mean it has to be kept permanently. My text message asking for milk might be considered evidence, but it has virtually no lasting value. Once the transaction is over and the milk is in the fridge, the question of accountability and proof vanishes. On the other hand, the ICO and Mueller reports are enduring records: sources of evidence with tremendous legal and operational value. Because they have such long-lasting value, we would say they are *archival*. We would want to keep the reports and much of the associated documentation permanently: as authoritative evidence of the activities, events, opinions, and decisions associated with the investigations.

Only a small portion of evidence is worth keeping permanently as archives. The US National Archives and Records Administration (NARA) operates on the principle—developed over many years and based on thorough research and analysis—that only 1 to 2 percent of all the records generated by the US government are worth preserving permanently. Even then, the volume of documentary evidence held by NARA is overwhelming: 10 billion pages of textual records; 12 million maps, charts, and architectural drawings; 25 million still photographs and graphics; 24 million aerial photographs; 300,000 reels of motion picture film; 400,000 video and sound recordings; and 133 terabytes of electronic data. (The 10 billion pages of documents alone are equivalent to 4.5 million copies of *Harry Potter and the Philosopher's Stone*.)[9]

No society can save more than the smallest portion of all the documentary sources it creates. Keeping too much just overwhelms us with extraneous information, obscuring the small, precious kernel of authentic and reliable proof.

The most important task is to distinguish the kernel worth keeping from the stuff surrounding it, and then to protect that valuable portion before it can be altered, deleted, or corrupted. But even if a documentary source has changed over time, it can still provide some evidential value, which means it is important to look not only at what is there but also at what might be missing. Gaps and silences in the documentary record are inevitable. But sometimes the absence of evidence *is* evidence. We can learn almost as much from what we don't see as what we do see, if we look hard enough.

Assessing Authenticity

When considering the trustworthiness of a proclamation signed by George Washington, we first must confirm the document is real. It could be a forgery, after all. We all know how many people on the Eastern Seaboard of the United States claim Washington slept in their second-best bedroom. Who knows how many people believe they have an original document signed by the Great Man?

We can attest to the authenticity of Washington's false proclamation when we see the original record in the Library of Congress in Washington, DC, where it has been preserved as part of George Washington's archives. Thanks to the efforts of archivists at the Library of Congress, we can also see a digital version of that document on the library's website. Even in digital form, George Washington's handwriting is visible, as is the date of the document and the official marks showing the proclamation was registered as part of Washington's correspondence. All the documentary elements—the signature line, address, and marginal notes—give the piece of paper a form and a structure that help us confirm its authenticity. It looks like other documents created or received by Washington at the same time, and it looks like other documents generated by other government officials at the time. It follows the "rules" of record making of the day. Even the paper and ink can be analyzed to estimate the date the record was made, giving us more assurance of its authenticity.[10]

Verifying the authenticity of digital evidence is much harder. When we look at emails, Twitter messages, or Instagram photographs, we need to look for contextual clues. Has a digital photograph been manipulated? Does the email address match the one we might expect to see from that sender? Is a tweet from a real Twitter account or an automated account (a bot)? Why did someone send the message to me? In the digital environment, we lose the traditional clues of form and structure. Our ability to trust digital sources is significantly lower for electronic records than for paper or analog materials because electronic records are so much easier to alter after the fact.

Determining Completeness

Documentary evidence is also more trustworthy when it is complete. Completeness doesn't mean the sentences have punctuation at the end. It means that we can confirm where the record came from, when it was created, and that it is intact. It is *all* there, whether *all* consists of a single handwritten letter, a collection of photographs in an album, a PDF copy of a report, or an entire series of emails on a subject.

What happens if we are faced with a torn sheet of paper showing George Washington's signature on the bottom with a few stray words above his name— "Given under my hand at the City of New York on the third day of November . . . blah blah blah"? This scrap of paper may be a charming curiosity, but it likely won't stand as proof of anything more than the fact that someone famous seems to have signed a piece of paper. Without the complete document and verification of authorship, it cannot serve as trustworthy proof of Washington's actions and decisions. All we have is his squiggled signature on a piece of cotton rag paper. (A valuable squiggle, perhaps, if the owner decides to sell it on eBay.)

To ensure the completeness of the ICO's report into Facebook and Cambridge Analytica or Mueller's report into Russian interference, we need to know we are seeing the whole report, from introduction to appendixes, with nothing missing. We would also benefit from seeing other documentary materials that give the report its context: press releases, emails and text messages, interview notes, witness statements, and so on.

What if a person saw only a few photocopied pages of one of these reports published on a third-party website? Or a partial copy of a government email about the reports, leaked to the press? What if the pages were so heavily redacted that all we could see was one or two white dots on a black background? What if there was no proof that the excerpt came from the original report, no guarantee that it was complete, and no assurance that it had not been changed? Verifying authenticity is one of the biggest challenges we face when documents are leaked to the public.

One of the best-known sources of leaked documents is WikiLeaks, founded in 2006. According to founder Julian Assange, WikiLeaks is not a rules breaker but is "a giant library" of what he calls "the world's most persecuted documents." As Assange argues, "We give asylum to these documents, we analyze them, we promote them, and we obtain more."[11] As of November 3, 2015 (the most recent update provided on the WikiLeaks website), WikiLeaks claimed that it had published more than 10 million documents, among them tens of thousands of emails and attachments taken from Hillary Clinton's private email server while she was secretary of state (which WikiLeaks claimed to have obtained through a Freedom of Information Act request).[12]

The process of formally submitting an access request to government does provide some assurance of authenticity, since the person requesting the documents and the government agency providing them must follow a prescribed set of rules and conditions. It is possible, when reviewing evidence provided from access requests, to know where the documents came from and how and when they were released. But the Clinton emails are not complete; they are only extracts from the whole of her official records as secretary of state, selected in order to answer a specific set of questions, which makes it difficult to know if we are seeing the right, best, or only evidence available. An access to information request answers a specific question. If someone asked to see only photographs with buildings in them or only letters written by unmarried women or only emails containing the word Christmas, that person would not see other evidence that might provide additional context. A selection of evidence does not tell the whole story.

When people remove sources of evidence from the official source, they are inevitably dealing with only a portion of a much larger whole. The challenge is magnified when evidence is not obtained through legal and formal channels. Leakers who obtain evidence not through access to information requests or other formal channels but through hacking into computers or receiving records stolen by others are acting without permission. They get what they can take, often without the intent, or ability, to consider whether what they get is the best evidence. How can we know that the leaked evidence is authentic and complete? How do we know whether there might be other evidence, not part of the leaked documents, that contradicts everything we see? And how much can we trust a leaker to make available for public scrutiny all the evidence he has obtained? What were the leaker's motivations?

Trustworthiness of evidence is compromised when the chain of evidence is broken. If someone in power is hiding the truth, then leaking evidence of her actions might be the best way to shine a light. But we must always look critically at what we see in that cache of leaked documents and ask ourselves, what is still missing?

Documenting Change

It is so easy to misinterpret evidence if it is taken out of context. One of the ways recordkeeping professionals preserve the authenticity and completeness of evidence is by preserving an unbroken chain of custody whenever possible. And if we cannot prevent breaks in the chain, we document those breaks whenever we can. First, we keep materials together in relation to the person or organization that created and used the evidence, a principle recordkeepers call *provenance*. Second, we keep materials in the order in which they were created, used, and stored, a principle we call *original order*. By documenting who created and used evidence, how that evidence was organized and reorganized over time, and whether there was any break in custody and care along the way, we can show what *ought* to be there, what *is* there, and *why* there might be gaps between the ideal and the reality.

In the ideal recordkeeping environment, the ICO and Mueller reports and all associated documentary materials would be captured as evidence as soon as they are created. No one would be allowed to change the final records; they would be frozen in time as trustworthy proof. In that same ideal world, George Washington's real-but-fake proclamation would continue to reside within the George Washington Papers, safe in the custody of nonpartisan, impartial archivists at the Library of Congress. In that ideal world, Hillary Clinton's emails would have been preserved in official State Department recordkeeping systems, and then in the safe hands of NARA, so that they would be available for public use as soon as legally possible. They would not have been kept on the Clinton family's personal email server, and no one at WikiLeaks would have felt compelled to publish copies.

Recordkeepers strive to ensure that the evidence in our care is authentic, complete, and unchanged. We prefer to participate from the beginning, when records are first made. But even if we step in later, our goal remains the same: to protect evidence as a source of trustworthy proof. As Canadian information management specialist John McDonald argues,

> Archivists don't pick up the residue of what has been produced through happenstance. They help, in a very sophisticated and non-intrusive way (kind of like the prime directive . . . which I know Captain Kirk would violate in just about every *Star Trek* episode) to help people have in place the records they would need to tell their story, assuming that emphasis would be placed on injecting, through a variety of means, all of those values that would respect the integrity and completeness of the records.[13]

Acknowledging Silences, Gaps, and Biases

Of course, even when evidence can be defined as authentic, complete, and unchanged, it may not be "true." A diary written by a colonial farmer presents his worldview, not necessarily that of his wife or of his children. A government surveyor might keep records of his efforts to map "uninhabited" areas; he might not be compelled to identify the homes or paths used by the aboriginal people living on the land he is marking for settlement. A photograph of a happy family in Victorian England might show five smiling children; missing is the family's disabled child, who was kept hidden from view.

As archivists David Thomas, Simon Fowler, and Valerie Johnson discuss in their fascinating analysis of the nature of archives, sometimes the silences are intentional. J. E. R. Parsons, imprisoned by the Japanese in World War II, kept a diary of his experiences in the camp, but as he recalled later, his account was less than honest. He knew that if the Japanese guards found the diary, they would punish him. To avoid that fate, he felt compelled to record "only those events to which the Japanese would not take too violent exception."[14]

Sometimes, archival silences and ostracism go hand in hand. In 1942, Jim Kepner, a journalist and author in California, began collecting publications, archives, and other historical material related to gay, lesbian, bisexual, and transgendered individuals and queer issues, even though same-sex sexual activity was still illegal in the United States. He secreted his collection in his apartment for decades, fearing the consequences if his archives were discovered. But as time passed his secret archives became more and more popular. In 1994, the University of Southern California acquired the archives, a fact that astonished Kepner, who recalled that for years mainstream society had been "our enemies."[15] Kepner died in 1997, having seen his archives go from a scattered group of secrets in his home to the largest collection of LGBTQ archives in the world.[16]

Sometimes silences and gaps emerge in sources of evidence because the people creating records in the first place have made assumptions about what is or is not worth documenting. For example, women are far less likely to be represented in archival materials from the 19th and early 20th centuries. It is not that women did not participate in society during those years. Rather, the evidence of their participation was often obscured by their perilous legal status. In England, married women were not allowed to own property or make wills until the 1880s. If you cannot own property, or leave your property to others, why would anyone create a record? In the United Kingdom, women were not eligible to vote until 1918; in the United States, they could not vote until 1920. Evidence of the political perspectives of women is not abundant: why document your views on government when you aren't allowed to participate in its creation? Even though thousands of women served as nurses, shipbuilders, and transport pilots in World War II, official records of their service are meager.

They were seen as temporary replacements for men, not legitimate members of the workforce. When someone's life and work are not valued, why document her experiences?[17]

It is impossible, really, to expect that sources of evidence will always be authentic or complete, or that every fact, event, or action ever undertaken will have been documented. Ignoring the context in which evidence was made, used, and kept diminishes the ability of a society to understand the complexity that lies behind our sense of truth and proof. Secrets and lies are part of life. Documentary sources of evidence are proof of life. Ergo, evidence can sometimes be proof of secrets and lies. No collection of documentary evidence is ever complete, and authenticity is not the same as honesty.

All sources of evidence need to be assessed not just for their ability to provide objective proof but also for their capacity to carry biases and perspectives. But accepting that evidence comes with a story does not mean that we should reject the evidence. Quite the contrary. We need to preserve all sorts of evidence, from all sectors of society, if we are going to have enough trustworthy proof to counter falsehoods and fictions. The recordkeeper's goal is not only to keep the "correct" evidence but to keep evidence that tells as many sides of a story as possible. In this regard, recordkeepers have tremendous power. Through our hands filters so much of the documentary evidence created by our societies. Our job is to defend, not to judge. This is one reason recordkeepers place so much emphasis on context. We cannot assess the evidential value of a collection of documentary sources without understanding the story behind the creation, management, and use of those sources.

But recordkeepers might not even have a chance to identify and protect trustworthy evidence if digital records and data have been altered, manipulated, or deleted before we can even assess them. We need to manage evidence from the start, so that people have access to all sorts of evidence, in all shapes and forms, to counter falsehoods and fictions with trustworthy proof.

NOTES

1. When it was ratified in 1790, the Constitution recognized that many of the people who might serve as US president in those early years might have been born elsewhere. The president could be a naturalized citizen "at the time of the Adoption of this Constitution," but today presidents must be "natural-born" Americans.

2. The official announcement related to the release of Obama's long-form birth certificate can be seen in a blog post by Dan Pfeiffer, "President Obama's Long Form Birth Certificate," Obama White House Archives, April 27, 2011, https://obamawhitehouse.archives.gov/blog/2011/04/27/president-obamas-long-form-birth-certificate, *archived at* https://perma.cc/R2YB-TC94.

3. The official reports, press releases, and other evidence associated with the ICO's investigation of Facebook and Cambridge Analytica can be found on the ICO website at https://ico.org.uk, *archived at* https://perma.cc/EN7U-LNYP. The final report by the Information Commissioner's Office, *Investigation into the Use of Data Analytics in Political Campaigns: A Report to Parliament* (ICO, November 6, 2018), is available at https://ico.org.uk/media/action-weve-taken/2260271/investigation-into-the-use-of-data-analytics-in-political-campaigns-final-20181105.pdf, *archived at* https://perma.cc/5GVS-7HYC.

4. Special Counsel Robert S. Mueller III's two-volume *Report on the Investigation into Russian Interference in the 2016 Presidential Election* (Washington, DC: US Department of Justice, March 2019), along with related court documents, is available for download on the US Department of Justice website at https://www.justice.gov/sco, *archived at* https://perma.cc/LQY3-MPVG. Because the DOJ version of the report was not searchable online when it was released on April 18, 2019, I used in my analysis the searchable version published by *The New York Times*, "Read the Mueller Report: Searchable Document and Index," *The New York Times*, April 18, 2019, https://www.nytimes.com/interactive/2019/04/18/us/politics/mueller-report-document.html, *archived at* https://perma.cc/GHN7-2AYF.

5. Cambridge Analytica was founded by Donald Trump's former White House Strategic Advisor Steve Bannon, with significant financial backing from Robert Mercer, an American hedge-fund manager and active conservative supporter. Facebook, launched by American Mark Zuckerberg in 2004, is one of the largest and most influential social media platforms in the world, with more than two billion users. As we are only just discovering with the release of these two reports, the British ICO report and the American Mueller report, the links between private consultants, social media companies, political operatives, and foreign governments are deep and troubling. The implications for the stability of democratic institutions, on both sides of the ocean, are grave.

6. For the Information Commissioner's comments about breaches of personal privacy, see Information Commissioner's Office, *Investigation into the Use of Data Analytics*, 5–6. Subsequent to the referendum, the UK government, under the leadership of Theresa May, invoked article 50 of the Treaty on European Union, triggering the countdown to the United Kingdom's departure. By the departure deadline of April 12, 2019, however, the government had not been able to confirm a withdrawal agreement, and May had to request an extension from the European Union, pushing the date for the United Kingdom's anticipated departure to October 31, 2019. Many analysts speculate that the door may be open to another referendum or a general election. Because the Brexit story is still so new, however, there are few objective analyses of events. The BBC has established a section on its website specifically dedicated to Brexit news and commentary, https://www.bbc.com/news/politics/uk_leaves_the_eu, *archived at* https://perma.cc/EDD2-C9ZT. Included

on this website is a valuable if still preliminary (and ever-changing) overview of events;

see Alex Hunt and Brian Wheeler, "Brexit: All You Need to Know about the UK Leaving the EU," *BBC News*, April 18, 2019, https://www.bbc.com/news/uk-politics -32810887, *archived at* https://perma.cc/CQR9-5BZL. A cogent explanation of the appropriation of Facebook data can be found at Andrew Prokop, "Cambridge Analytica Shutting Down: The Firm's Many Scandals, Explained," *Vox*, May 2, 2018, https://www.vox.com/policy-and-politics/2018/3/21/17141428/cambridge -analytica-trump-russia-mueller, *archived at* https://perma.cc/NFB4-PZ5B.

7. Trump repeated his claim of "no collusion, no obstruction" many times in the lead-up to the release of the Mueller report, including the day the report was released. See Christina Wilkie, "Trump Responds to Mueller Report: 'No Collusion, No Obstruction,'" CNBC.com, "Politics," April 18, 2019, https://www.cnbc.com/ 2019/04/18/trump-responds-to-mueller-report-no-collusion-no-obstruction.html, *archived at* https://perma.cc/9DKX-BT88. For Mueller's statement about Russian interference and his concluding statement, see Mueller, *Report on Russian Interference*, vol. I, p. 1, and vol. II, p. 182, respectively. A summary of the key findings of the report, produced the day the report was released, is Olivia Paschal and Madeleine Carlisle, "14 Must-Read Moments from the Mueller Report," *The Atlantic*, April 18, 2019, https://www.theatlantic.com/politics/archive/2019/ 04/mueller-report-release-barr-trump/587176/?utm_source=newsletter&utm _medium=email&utm_campaign=politics-daily-newsletter&utm_content=2019 0418&silverid-ref=NDI2MTczNTkxNTkyS0, *archived at* https://perma.cc/2C3Z -GCKD.

8. Questions have already swirled about the way in which the Mueller report was disseminated—or not. William Barr, the attorney general who received the report on March 24, 2019, took the unprecedented step of not making the report available to Congress or the public for 25 days after it was submitted to his office. He also expanded the criteria for redaction beyond those categories normally accepted for such reports. As knowledge management expert Steve Denning reported, the attorney general's actions were considered by many in government to be deeply problematic, if not actually suspicious. See Steve Denning, "Why Barr's Delay in Releasing the Mueller Report Is Unprecedented and Unreasonable," *Forbes,* March 31, 2019, https://www.forbes.com/sites/stevedenning/2019/03/31/why-barrs -delay-in-releasing-the-mueller-report-is-unprecedented-and-unreasonable/#5795 de144a40, *archived at* https://perma.cc/Y79A-PPXT.

9. For more information on NARA and its holdings and operations, including a discussion of NARA's estimate of the percentage of records worth keeping permanently, see the NARA website at https://www.archives.gov/about, *archived at* https:// perma.cc/F9CN-MLPG.

10. The Library of Congress finding aid for the George Washington Papers can be seen at http://findingaids.loc.gov/db/search/xq/searchMfer02.xq?_id=loc.mss.eadmss .ms008068&_faSection=overview&_faSubsection=did&_dmdid, *archived at* https:// perma.cc/KJ98-HBXM.

11. "We Are Drowning in Material," interview of Julian Assange by Germany's Michael

Sontheimer, *Spiegel Online*, July 20, 2015, http://www.spiegel.de/international/world/spiegel-interview-with-wikileaks-head-julian-assange-a-1044399.html, *archived at* https://perma.cc/HE9U-3WZU.

12. See the official WikiLeaks "Hillary Clinton Email Archive" page at https://wikileaks.org/clinton-emails, *archived at* https://perma.cc/VT6V-M69T.

13. Email communication with John McDonald, June 28, 2018.

14. J. E. R. Parsons, quoted in David Thomas, Simon Fowler, and Valerie Johnson, *The Silence of the Archive* (London: Facet, 2017), 43.

15. Myrna Oliver, "Jim Kepner; Pioneer Activist Founded Gay Archives in 1942" (obituary), *LA Times*, November 18, 1997, http://articles.latimes.com/1997/nov/18/news/mn-55007, *archived at* https://perma.cc/3EFV-MCJP.

16. See the ONE Archives Foundation website at www.onearchives.org/about, *archived at* https://perma.cc/P2X5-RTJ3.

17. For an analysis of the role and visibility of women in archives, see the discussion in Thomas, Fowler, and Johnson, *Silence of the Archive*, esp. 46–47. Also of interest are Kate Eichhorn, *The Archival Turn in Feminism: Outrage in Order* (Philadelphia: Temple University Press, 2013), and Gabrielle Durepos, Alan McKinlay, and Scott Taylor, "Narrating Histories of Women at Work: Archives, Stories, and the Promise of Feminism," *Business History* 59, no. 8 (2017): 1261–79.

4

"Talking knots"

The Form of Evidence

Today when we want to get our bearings in our own culture, and have need to stand aside from the bias and pressure exerted by any technical form of human expression, we have only to visit a society where that particular form has not been felt, or a historical period in which it was unknown.

Marshall McLuhan, 1964

ON AUGUST 6, 1945, THE CITY OF HIROSHIMA, JAPAN, WAS HIT BY AN atomic bomb. Over 80,000 people were killed almost immediately. Three days later, 18-year-old Toru Sato, who had been out of Hiroshima Prefecture at the time of the bombing, returned to the city to look for his family. As he searched the ruins of his family home, Toru discovered a roof tile on the ground. Some characters were barely visible on the surface, scratched by a knife, perhaps, or a stone. They read, "Sato family, Atsuko well, Kuniko dead, Father, Tatsumi, Kazue unknown."[1]

This tile may be the only recorded evidence left of the Sato family's documentary story. Everything else—family photographs, letters to grandparents, marriage certificates—would have been incinerated at 8:16 a.m. that August day. Archivists may seek a "whole" body of records, but we accept the reality that even the smallest scrap can serve as evidence. This solitary tile *is* the story.

Under normal circumstances, most people do not capture evidence in a roof tile. But ever since people began storing information in recorded form, they have used the tools available to them at that moment, whether pen and parchment or keyboard and computer. Evidence can be made of magnetic tape, fiber, wood, or electronic signals; it can be a song or a story.

Evidence is a social construct, just like financial currencies or geopolitical boundaries. There is no "right" way to create a record. People will decide what they will document, how they will document it, and why they will document it, according to their own needs, technologies, politics, cultures, and customs. The challenge is not just to preserve the evidence, regardless of its form, but also to ensure it can be understood and used now and for as long as humanly possible. Sometimes that challenge is overwhelming.

Decoding Symbols

Deep inside caves across Europe are paintings that date back tens of thousands of years. Some images depict animals, humans, weapons, or tools. Others are symbols, such as triangles, circles, and lines. Are they evidence of hunting activities, religious offerings, or spiritual visions? Are they an ancient form of graffiti? Paleoanthropologist Genevieve von Petzinger has studied the cave paintings and identified a total of 32 distinct graphic symbols—circles, lines, spirals, zigzags, and so on—which she believes represent intentional choices. They seem to be a form of language, common across thousands of miles. But we do not know the message they convey.[2]

We may not understand the paintings on cave walls, but we do know what the symbols on the Rosetta Stone mean. In 1799, the stone, a type of igneous rock called "granodiorite," was uncovered by one of Napoléon Bonaparte's soldiers. The stone, it turned out, communicated the same message in three different languages: Egyptian hieroglyphics, Greek lettering, and an Egyptian form of writing known as Demotic script. But the only known language was Greek, and even then, some of the symbols were mysterious. In the early 1800s, British polymath Thomas Young and French philologist Jean-François Champollion worked separately to decode the symbols, discovering that the stone was a decree issued in Memphis, in Lower Egypt, in 196 BC. It confirmed priestly support for King Ptolemy V. Deciphering the Rosetta Stone not only made the decree intelligible but also allowed people to decipher other stones carved with one of the same languages, bringing to life a multitude of previously silent sources of evidence.[3]

Scholars have had more difficulty understanding the purpose and meaning of the quipu, a form of record used in the Andean region of South America from around 1100 to 1500 AD. The quipu, also known as "talking knots," consists of a series of fiber cords, each tied into knots. A single quipu could include as many as 2,000 cords, in different colors and with different numbers of knots. Eventually, researchers deduced that the knots represented numbers, based on a decimal system, and they have suggested that the quipu served as a record of financial transactions. Some believe that the quipu might have been used to record census information, and still others think the knots might have been used to capture literary information. No one knows for sure.[4]

Researchers have had more success interpreting the English split tally stick or "nick stick," common from about the 12th century. A piece of willow or hazel was marked with a series of notches; each notch represented a number related to the amount of a debt owed or payment made. Once the notches were carved, the stick was split in half lengthwise. Each half served as a record of the transaction. If one party added lines to his half of the stick, the notches would not align when the halves were brought together. Thus the stick served as a trustworthy record.[5]

Today, we can only guess at the general nature and purpose of these ancient records. They are interesting and informative, certainly, but their value as evidence of specific transactions is diminished because we are missing so much contextual information.

Interpreting Documents

Interpreting evidence becomes easier after the fall of the Western Roman Empire, when European records at least began to look a bit more like we are used to now, made with languages, not codes. As well, record *making* became more commonplace as literacy spread. Ladies of the manor kept personal diaries; businessmen filled the pages of financial ledgers; explorers penned logbooks of their travels; and soldiers wrote letters home to their families. As more people learned how to read and write, agreements notched on pieces of wood were replaced by written statements saying, "I owe you 10 shillings and not a farthing more."[6]

If we want to make sense of these documents, of course, we still need to understand their language, culture, and context. When the wool merchant Thomas Betson wrote a love letter to his fiancée Katherine Riche in 1476, he sent her his love, recommending to her "all the inwardnesse of myn hart" and praying that "Almyghty Jhesu make you a good woman, and send you many good yeres and longe to lyveffe in helth and vertu to his plesour."[7] Betson's letter is not as indecipherable as a cave painting, but making sense of it six centuries after the fact is still not a straightforward exercise.

Two centuries later, the Civil War brought us another documentary bounty, as photographic technologies emerged. People would buy *cartes-de-visite* or stereographs (a form of 3-D image) depicting soldiers and equipment. These were the postcards of the day. Newspapers published images of battlefields, often only days after the battle had ended.[8]

But Civil War photographs are not straightforward sources of evidence. Photographic equipment was cumbersome, and a single exposure could take up to

30 seconds. Capturing images of soldiers in action was technically impossible. Photographers who wanted to show some of the gritty reality of the war might move bodies, rearrange objects, or add debris in order to portray a more evocative scene. The photographs are authentic, in that they show us contemporary images of a time and place, but their measure of truth is a matter of perspective. They present a view, a bias perhaps, but they still tell us something important about the war. Our job is to interpret such evidence in its context, not reject it out of hand.[9]

Addressing the Evidence Boom

The 20th century saw the creation of even more record-making tools and technologies, resulting in an explosion in both the form and volume of evidence. From the invention of Kodak's first box camera in 1888, promoted with the slogan "You press the button, we do the rest," personal photography became much simpler. Soon anyone from a professional photographer to a ten-year-old kid could take pictures in a multitude of shapes and forms: black and white, color, Instamatic, Polaroid, print, or slide. And as moving-image equipment became portable and affordable, the average person could own and operate a movie camera. Anyone born before 1960 probably remembers being collared by the parents and told to Walk and Wave, Walk and Wave, as Dad captured the family's camping holiday in stunning Super 8.

Audio recordings were first produced in the 1850s, but it was not until Thomas Edison created a cylinder-based phonograph in 1878 that sound could really be captured and shared easily. By 1929 the flat disc had replaced the cylinder. Magnetic tape appeared in the late 1920s; multitrack recording in the 1940s; video-recording technologies in the 1950s; and cassette tapes in the early 1960s. Today there are hundreds of different audio-recording devices in existence, along with over 50 different videotape formats. (And I remember when deciding whether to go with Beta or VHS was a struggle.)

As audiovisual technologies became easier to use, a new documentary form emerged. Sound and moving images were captured to support history, anthropology, genealogy, or other endeavors. Real-time recordings of live events provided evidence of traditional songs, legends, dances, or ceremonies. Oral history interviews, on the other hand, were constructed events: the interviewer and interviewee both recognized they were telling a story. As people began conducting oral history interviews, the authenticity of the final documentary product could be challenged. We all react differently when we know the "Record" button is on.

But oral history interviews, recordings of live performances, and other audiovisual recordings, while they might sit on the border between objective proof and subjective interpretation, form an integral part of any collection of documentary evidence. They give us voices and faces and sounds, instead of just words on a page. As Mark Piva, Assistant Director of Oral History and Folklore at the National Library of Australia, says, "Oral history not only gives you the story, but a rich sense of the person behind the story."[10]

Technology also changed the nature, scope, and volume of the written word. Typewriters replaced handwriting, and secretaries replaced monks and scribes. Eventually, keyboards replaced typewriters, then smartphones and tablets appeared. With each change in technology, the volume of documentary output grew, seemingly exponentially. In 1912, the accumulation of US government records was about 60,000 cubic feet a year, a volume that would fill about 2/3 of an Olympic swimming pool. By 1930 that volume had expanded to 200,000 cubic feet a year, or more than 2 swimming pools. By 1968 the US government was generating 4 million cubic feet of records a year, filling more than 45 swimming pools.[11]

When computers became common, and people could keep their "office" with them 24/7, the volume and diversity of communications grew and grew. It has been estimated that in 2018, more than 281 billion business emails were sent around the world every day. If we converted all those emails into paper form and put them into swimming pools, New York City would sink.[12]

Dealing with Data

I have argued that data, information, and evidence are not the same thing. But this is not necessarily true in a digital age. Certainly, a piece of raw data taken out of context cannot prove anything. "8" is uncontextualized data. But "8 planets" is information. A report by the International Astronomical Union explaining why there are 8 planets instead of 9 is evidence of the research behind the decision to demote Pluto. The fact is, data elements can have evidential value, if one can put the different data elements into context, to allow them to serve as verifiable facts.

What if we saw the number 180 in a database? That number could mean anything. My husband's weight. The speed at which a car is driving on the highway. The year Roman Emperor Marcus Aurelius died. But what if the number 180 is linked to a data field labeled "CD4 Count"? Now the number has a particular meaning. A CD4 count is an estimate of the number of CD4 or white blood cells in a person's body; the number is often used to assess a person's ability to fight off viruses such as HIV. The higher the number, the better a person's immune system is working. The normal range for CD4 cells is 500–1,500. If a person's CD4 count drops below 200, that person has a seriously compromised immune system and would likely be diagnosed with AIDS.

Imagine for a moment a hypothetical patient and her hypothetical doctor. What if that raw number, 180, sits in a database at that doctor's office, in a data field labeled CD4 Count? Another data field in the same database captures the patient's name, and other data fields capture the patient's address, age, and sex. Left separately, the data fields are just words and numbers: Oklahoma, Alicia, Main Street, 42, Tulsa, 1234, female, Graham. Put together, the data provide evidence that our hypothetical patient, Alicia Graham, is a 42-year-old female living at 1234 Main Street, Tulsa, Oklahoma. The data also provide evidence that Alicia has a CD4 count of 180. She very likely has AIDS. The number 180 now serves as evidence. Verifiable evidence about an identifiable person.

Alicia Graham and her doctor need to know this number. Her medical treatment depends on it. Who else needs to know? An insurance broker? An employer? Alicia's neighbors? To protect the authenticity of that number, and to protect Alicia's privacy, her doctor needs to ensure the number is entered into the database accurately, that it is stored securely, and that it is accessible to only those who have the right to see it. If the data had been gathered in paper form, it would sit in a file, locked in the doctor's filing cabinet or copied onto a document for Alicia to keep in her own medical file. Today, this highly personal data, this source of evidence, sits on a computer server, which may not even be in the same city, state, or country as Alicia and her doctor.

What if Alicia Graham's CD4 count was changed as a result of a computer malfunction or altered by a malicious hacker? What if the database showed 800 instead of 180? Who would know it was wrong? Alicia could go without critical medical care because the evidence of her medical condition was not accurate. Her diagnosis could be shared with people she would prefer did not know. Surely Alicia has the right to know that this evidence about her, whether it lives in a paper file or a digital database, is authentic, complete, unchanged, and *private*. (Of course, the paper record could also be compromised, but changes to physical documents are not as easy, and certainly not as invisible, as alterations to digital evidence.)

This hypothetical example leads us to the scandal that surrounds the story of foreign interference in elections and referenda, including the Facebook/Cambridge Analytica case in the United Kingdom and the Russian interference case in the United States. In both countries, malicious actors such as foreign agents or political operatives accessed data about people, particularly data on social media tools such as Facebook, without their explicit permission. These actors then used the data—the evidence—in an attempt to manipulate opinions and voting patterns.

In the UK situation, Cambridge Analytica ended up harvesting vast reams of personal evidence from Facebook pages, capitalizing on a loophole in Facebook's privacy settings that maintained a default "opt in" agreement. According to this agreement, personal information from someone's Facebook page could be shared with anyone Facebook chose, even though the person in question had not given explicit permission to share such information. As noted by one of the data scientists who mined data for Cambridge Analytica, this vague permission statement "seems crazy now" but was "a core feature of the Facebook platform for years."[13]

Cambridge Analytica then employed algorithms ("rules" that tell the computer how to interpret data) to decode the evidence gleaned from the Facebook pages. The company could then use that decoded evidence for a whole range of reasons. Anytime someone posted a photograph, "liked" a particular product, or shared a post about politics or his church or her community group, that person was sharing personal evidence, which Cambridge Analytica could then use to "microtarget" people: directing specific political advertisements to different groups of people to sway their opinions and influence their votes.[14]

According to the Mueller report, Russian operatives used Facebook similarly in the United States, in an attempt to sway voters during the 2016 American election. Russian agents set up Facebook accounts and directed advertisements to specific people or groups, who had been identified through an analysis of personal Facebook pages. The agents then disseminated anti-Clinton messages, including a March 18, 2016 advertisement showing Clinton along with a caption that read, in part, "If one day God lets this liar enter the White House as a president—that day would be a real national tragedy." Other Facebook ads showed Clinton with a black cross over her face, and some showed images of people holding guns, urging viewers to defend the constitutional amendment supporting the right to bear arms.[15]

When Thomas Betson wrote his fiancée Katherine Riche, sending "all the inwardnesse of myn hart," he probably never imagined that anyone other than Katherine or he might see that letter. If his protestations of love were posted on Facebook today, how many complete strangers could give Tom and Kathy the thumbs-up? And are those thumbs evidence? If reports into the use and misuse of social media in the United States and United Kingdom are anything to go by, they are.

Coping with the Deluge

As I noted earlier, in 1912 the US government generated about 60,000 cubic feet of records, and in 1968 it produced 4 million cubic feet of records. During Bill Clinton's tenure as president, from 1993 to 2001, his office created or received 32 million presidential and federal emails. That's just email messages, not reports or memos or briefing papers, and that is just from the Office of the President, not any other part of government. When George W. Bush was president, from 2001 to 2009, the number of emails coming from his office grew to more than 200 million. By the time of Barack Obama's tenure, from 2009 to 2017, that number had grown to more than 300 million. If only 1 to 2 percent of the records made by a government have enduring value, how much are we keeping now? Do we keep 3 million emails out of 300 million? Which ones contain critical evidence? Which ones are lunch invitations? Was the lunch part of a political meeting with a world leader? A working meal with a member of the cabinet? A midday tryst with a White House intern? Finding the essential core of authentic, enduring evidence in the phenomenal volume of digital content, and then preserving that core before it has been lost to a power outage, malicious hack, or computer virus, while ensuring the other millions of communications are destroyed securely, is perhaps the greatest evidential challenge we face in the 21st century.[16]

Returning to Symbols

Technology never stops changing. Today, reports are published electronically rather than in print. Email, once such a groundbreaking form of communication, is now derided as formal and antiquated. As fewer people write "old fashioned" letters, post offices around the world, many of them state-sponsored and subsidized, are going bankrupt. Instruction manuals are out; do-it-yourself YouTube videos are in.

Despite its recent brush with notoriety, Facebook is still the most popular social media platform in the world, used by some 2.32 billion people every month.[17] Twitter, which allows people to send short bursts of information in 280-character tweets, is used by more than 300 million people. Celebrities confess their marital infidelities on Twitter. Law firms issue subpoenas on Twitter. Presidents and prime ministers release policy statements on Twitter. Some of those tweets serve as crucial sources of recorded evidence.[18]

Some people don't even write words anymore. Of the almost 3,000 different Unicode Standard emoji symbols in use today, the most popular is :

a person shrugging. (Maybe the shrug indicates that the person has no idea what the other emojis mean.) What if, instead of sending my husband a text message to ask for milk, I sent the following?

Today, Thomas Betson wouldn't write Katherine Riche "all the inwardnesse of myn hart." He would post to her Facebook time line.

Cracking New Codes

Science is pushing the boundaries even further. In 2018, researchers from the University of Washington, working with specialists at Microsoft Research, stored 400 megabytes of data by encoding it into a microscopic string of DNA. They were later able to retrieve the data without errors. In another experiment, scientists successfully transplanted memories from one snail to another. (Now data can move fast and slow at the same time.)[19] We have no idea what the future of evidence will be. But if societies wish to remember outside of their own minds and hearts, they will always find new and different ways to capture sources of proof in some discrete, tangible form.

Among the 130,000 clay tablets preserved in the British Museum is a small tablet from southern Iraq, no bigger than a computer mouse. The pictographs on the tablet document the distribution of beer rations to workers in the Mesopotamian city-state of Uruk. Even though hardened clay is an extremely stable medium, museum staff periodically "recook" the tablets in a specially designed kiln in order to keep them from crumbling. The management and preservation of digital evidence demand the same ongoing commitment, but the challenge is harder because the tools we think are commonplace today could be obsolete in months, never mind centuries. How does one "recook" a data element, I wonder?[20]

Evidence is a social construct. We decide what it will look like and why it should be created and kept. And then we become dependent on that evidence, whatever its form, as our source of proof. As renowned archival thinker Geoffrey Yeo argues, "The world shapes the form and function of records; at the same time, by co-ordinating human behaviour, establishing rights and responsibilities, or creating social relations, records play a role in shaping the world."[21]

Evidence once took the form of quipu, clay tablets, and print photographs. Recordkeeping specialists have had to figure out how to capture, preserve, and interpret these different forms of evidence, sometimes with limited success. Today, we capture documentary proof using CDs, magnetic tape, and cloud-based storage systems. Up next are DNA strings and snails. Through it all, recordkeepers focus not just on the form of the evidence but also on its purpose and on its potential value for a wide variety of uses. To discern that value, we need to understand how the evidence came to be, what it says, what it means, why it was created, and how it was used. Today, we cannot wait decades or centuries to decode digital evidence. If we do, we could face a documentary mystery as elusive as knotted threads or triangles on a wall.

NOTES

1. The tile can be seen in the virtual museum of the Hiroshima Peace Memorial Museum, at http://www.pcf.city.hiroshima.jp/virtual/index_e.html, *archived at* https://perma.cc/8ME8-5ZC3.

2. See Genevieve von Petzinger, *The First Signs: Unlocking the Mysteries of the World's Oldest Symbols* (New York: Atria Books, 2016).

3. See John Ray, *The Rosetta Stone and the Rebirth of Ancient Egypt* (Boston: Harvard University Press, 2012). The catalog description for the Rosetta Stone can be found on the British Museum website at http://www.britishmuseum.org/research/collection_online/collection_object_details.aspx?objectId=117631&partId=1, *archived at* https://perma.cc/5PNF-QPVT.

4. See Gary Urton, *Inka History in Knots: Reading Khipus as Primary Sources* (Austin: University of Texas Press, 2017).

5. A description of the nature and purpose of tally sticks can be found on the British Library website at https://www.bl.uk/collection-items/tally-sticks, *archived at* https://perma.cc/9N4R-5K8M, with additional information at https://www.bl.uk/collection-items/~/link.aspx?_id=B0C190B5960A41B893B847361F7E64F7&_z=z, *archived at* https://perma.cc/DU2M-M3X9. Interestingly, there is a direct link between tally sticks and the establishment of a formal archival service in England. Tally sticks were regularly destroyed by the British government once they were no longer needed, sometimes by burning them in an outside bonfire or by giving them away as firewood. When the Palace of Westminster decided to burn a large quantity of obsolete sticks in its furnaces on October 16, 1834, the resulting fire burned down a number of government buildings. Fortunately, the winds blew away from other records storage areas, ensuring official government documents were not lost, but in the aftermath officials decided a secure repository was needed. The Public Record Office was opened in 1838. See John D. Cantwell, *The Public Record Office, 1838–1958* (London: HMSO, 1991). Up-to-date information about the Palace of Westminster can also be found on the official website for the UK Parliament at https://www.parliament.uk/about/living-heritage/building/palace/estatehistory/

from-the-parliamentary-collections/fire-of-westminster/tallysticks, *archived at* https://perma.cc/9RPV-PVXB.

6. For a detailed analysis of the nature and evolution of medieval records, see Michael Clanchy, *From Memory to Written Record: England 1066–1307*, 3rd ed. (Chichester, UK: Wiley-Blackwell, 2012).

7. Betson's words translate to modern English as "all the inwardness of my heart" and "Almighty Jesus make you a good woman, and send you many good years and long life and health and virtue to His pleasure." His letter is transcribed and contextualized in Charles Lethbridge Kingsford's edition of *The Stonor Letters and Papers, 1290–1483; ed. for the Royal Historical Society, from the Original Documents in the Public Record Office* (London: Royal Historical Society, 1919). The online edition was produced as part of the Corpus of Middle English Prose and Verse by the University of Michigan; see http://name.umdl.umich.edu/ACA1723.0001.001, *archived at* https://perma.cc/KT7X-8DHV.

8. Thousands of Civil War photographs survived and are now housed in institutions such as the Library of Congress and the National Archives in Washington, DC, and in state and local repositories across the country. Civil War photographs can also be seen on the NARA website at https://www.archives.gov/research/military/civil-war/photos, *archived at* https://perma.cc/9ZT2-A2E7, and on the Library of Congress website at http://www.loc.gov/pictures/item/94837685, *archived at* https://perma.cc/ZR54-L3DX. Also of interest is the Center for Civil War Photography at https://www.civilwarphotography.org, *archived at* https://perma.cc/5KBT-GM4E.

9. See William C. Davis, *The Civil War in Photographs* (London: Carlton Books, 2013), and J. Matthew Gallman and Gary W. Gallagher, *Lens of War: Exploring Iconic Photographs of the Civil War* (Athens: University of Georgia Press, 2015).

10. Meeting with Mark Piva, National Library of Australia, December 4, 2018.

11. See H. G. Jones, *The Records of a Nation* (New York: Atheneum, 1969), esp. 8–9.

12. For early US government statistics, see Jones, *Records of a Nation*. For email statistics, see Heinz Tschabitscher, "The Number of Emails Sent per Day in 2018 (and 20+ Other Email Facts)," *Lifewire*, September 9, 2018, https://www.lifewire.com/how-many-emails-are-sent-every-day-1171210, *archived at* https://perma.cc/96LV-CBVX.

13. See "Aleksandr Kogan: The Link between Cambridge Analytica and Facebook," interview by Lesley Stahl, CBS's *60 Minutes*, April 22, 2018, https://www.cbsnews.com/news/aleksandr-kogan-the-link-between-cambridge-analytica-and-facebook, *archived at* https://perma.cc/6JPX-9WTV. Facebook claims to have closed the privacy loophole, after it was discovered that the previous default agreement between Facebook and its users allowed Facebook to access information about people's friends without explicit permission. Many data experts now contend that Facebook and Cambridge Analytica are responsible for a grave breach of privacy laws.

14. Cathy O'Neil offers insightful commentary on Facebook and algorithms in *Weapons of Math Destruction: How Big Data Increases Inequality and Threatens Democracy* (London: Penguin, 2017).

15. See Special Counsel Robert S. Mueller III, *Report on the Investigation into Russian Interference in the 2016 Presidential Election* (Washington, DC: US Department of Justice, March 2019), vol. I, p. 25, https://www.justice.gov/sco, *archived at* https:// perma.cc/LQY3-MPVG, as published by *The New York Times* at https://www.nytimes .com/interactive/2019/04/18/us/politics/mueller-report-document.html, *archived at* https://perma.cc/GHN7-2AYF. See also the samples of advertisements posted in 2018 on the Democrat's section of the website for the US House of Representatives Permanent Select Committee on Intelligence at https://democrats-intelligence .house.gov/social-media-content, *archived at* https://perma.cc/C52A-7QS5.

16. See Jason Barron, *The Impact of NARA's E-mail Capstone Policy and Other Recent Initiatives on FOIA Access* (Freedom of Information Act Advisory Committee, October 19, 2017), https://www.archives.gov/files/Baron-foia-advisory-committee -presentation.pdf, *archived at* https://perma.cc/TMV3-V33A. See also NARA, *White Paper on the Capstone Approach and Capstone GRS* (April 2015), https://www .archives.gov/files/records-mgmt/email-management/final-capstone-white-paper .pdf, *archived at* https://perma.cc/LV7W-6LQM.

17. See the Statista analysis of Facebook users in 2018 at https://www.statista.com/ statistics/264810/number-of-monthly-active-facebook-users-worldwide, *archived at* https://perma.cc/4VDS-YX6E. Ironically, younger generations seem to be fleeing Facebook much faster than their elders. In 2018, only 51 percent of teenagers said they used Facebook, down from 71 percent in 2015. Instead, more teenagers turned to YouTube (85 percent), Instagram (72 percent), and Snapchat (69 percent). Perhaps it is not a question of trust but a matter of preference. Teenagers go where their grandparents don't go. And their grandparents, it seems, love Facebook. See Olivia Solon, "Teens Are Abandoning Facebook in Dramatic Numbers, Study Finds," *The Guardian*, June 1, 2018, https://www.theguardian.com/ technology/2018/jun/01/facebook-teens-leaving-instagram-snapchat-study-user -numbers, *archived at* https://perma.cc/YV52-H6S2. See also Anthony Cuthbertson, "Facebook Is Officially for Old People," *Newsweek*, February 12, 2018, https:// www.newsweek.com/facebook-officially-old-people-803196, *archived at* https:// perma.cc/S4GF-JPNA.

18. On August 9, 2018, lawyers representing the Democratic National Committee (DNC) served WikiLeaks with papers related to a lawsuit, accusing WikiLeaks of working with Donald Trump's campaign and Russia to influence the 2016 presidential election. The papers were served via Twitter after the lawyers were unable to serve WikiLeaks using other methods. See John Bowden, "WikiLeaks Hit with DNC Lawsuit—Over Twitter," *The Hill*, August 10, 2018, http://thehill.com/ policy/technology/401324-wikileaks-hit-with-dnc-lawsuit-over-twitter, *archived at* https://perma.cc/M5BN-ZJG8. See also Kathryn Watson, "DNC Serves WikiLeaks with Lawsuit via Twitter," *CBS News*, August 10, 2018, https://www.cbsnews .com/news/dnc-serves-wikileaks-with-lawsuit-via-twitter, *archived at* https:// perma.cc/74CK-XBEZ. As I note later, when Robert Mueller and his team investigated links between WikiLeaks and Russian operatives, they uncovered multiple instances where WikiLeaks leaked stolen emails in order to damage Hillary Clinton's campaign. They also found evidence of ongoing communications between

WikiLeaks representatives and the Russian agents involved in election interference. See Mueller, *Report on Russian Interference*, vol. I, esp. 44–49.

19. Shivani Dave, "'Memory Transplant' Achieved in Snails," *BBC News*, May 14, 2018, https://www.bbc.com/news/science-environment-44111476, *archived at* https://perma.cc/5CBT-8CZH. See also Christine Kenneally, *The Invisible History of the Human Race* (New York: Viking, 2014).

20. The podcast and details of the artifact are available on the BBC's A History of the World website; see *A History of the World in 100 Objects*, "Early Writing Tablet," http://www.bbc.co.uk/ahistoryoftheworld/objects/TnAQ0B8bQkSJzKZFWo6F-g, *archived at* https://perma.cc/8UWF-2V8Z.

21. Geoffrey Yeo, *Records, Information, and Data* (London: Facet, 2018), 152.

5

"Let the other side be heard"

Evidence, Identity, and Connection

I am part of all that I have met.
Alfred, Lord Tennyson, 1833

A SOLDIER WRITES HOME TO HIS MOTHER, BROTHER, AND SISTER, saying, "I pray that you are in good health night and day." But, he adds, "I am worried about you because although you received letters from me often, you never wrote back to me." He says he has written six letters home with no reply. All we know of this soldier is that his name was Aurelius Polion, that he was an Egyptian solider serving in a Roman legion somewhere in Europe, and that he wrote the letter sometime in the second century AD.[1]

I have no Roman blood, but when I read this letter from nearly two millennia ago, I feel a connection. This soldier reminds me of my father, who served in World War II and wrote home to his mother from North Africa, and my grandfather, who served in World War I and wrote home to *his* mother from France.

Recorded evidence helps us feel a sense of connection with family, country, and world. Our parents' letters and diaries remind us that they were young once; photographs of our grandparents help us forge links with people we might never have met. Newspaper accounts and line drawings of our town in 1855 remind us that people walked the same paths as we hundreds of years before our birth. When people have a sense of identity and community, they might just feel that they have a greater stake in their society.

When people cannot make those connections, what happens to their sense of belonging? Do they care if the roads in their town deteriorate, if businesses disrespect local laws, or if gangs terrorize unsuspecting residents? It might seem a long path from archival documents to gang violence. But recorded evidence reminds us that we are part of an ongoing story—that life did not begin the moment our feet landed on Planet Earth. If we have a greater appreciation of the lives and work of our ancestors, maybe we will also care a little more about the fate of our descendants?

Tracing Blood Lines

I am one of the millions who pay to access the Ancestry.com genealogical database in search of my family history. Some years ago, my husband and I visited several World War I battle sites in Europe, and on our return home to Canada, I grew curious about my grandfather's wartime experience. I signed up with Ancestry, admittedly with some reservations. (Anyone married to a direct descendent of Benedict Arnold is bound to pull the short straw in the genealogy game.) But I took the plunge.

Imagine my surprise—shock would be a better word—to discover that not only had my grandfather served in World War I but so had his three brothers. I didn't know he had three brothers. One of them, my Great Uncle Frank, was killed in action in 1916, aged 27. He was buried at the Railway Dugouts Burial Ground near Zillebeke, Belgium. I had no idea that Great Uncle Frank had died. I had no idea that Great Uncle Frank had lived.

The information on the Ancestry portal confirmed Great Uncle Frank's death. But Uncle Frank came to life for me when I read his 52-page service record, preserved by Library and Archives Canada. Reading the file, I learned that Great Uncle Frank began as a private with the 49th Battalion of the Canadian Expeditionary Force. He was treated for gastritis in 1915 and again in 1916. He was diagnosed with shell shock on May 1, 1916, but returned to duty a week later. Then, on August 5, 1916, at the Battle of the Somme, he was killed in action. His mother received $17.00 in back pay when his accounts were reconciled.

Only a year before I saw his file, I had been holidaying just a few miles from where he was buried. Of course, I didn't stop. How can you visit the grave of someone you don't know is there? Imagine: at 9:00 a.m. one morning I had no Great Uncle Frank; by 5:00 p.m. that evening, after seeing dozens of pages of documentary evidence, I was in tears, feeling I had disrespected his memory by not visiting him.

The Ancestry database is a wondrous tool. But none of the evidence in the Ancestry database would exist if it had not been preserved in an archival institution. People love to say they found "lost" archives, "hidden" from view, "buried" in the depths of an archival repository. The reality is, the evidence is not lost. It is not hidden. It is not buried. Records like my Great Uncle Frank's service file are just lying quietly, in safe storage, waiting for someone like me to come and use them.[2]

One of the reasons I could see the evidence of Great Uncle Frank, from my home thousands of miles west of Library and Archives Canada, was that staff at the institution have been working since 2014 to digitize its Personnel Records of the First World War collection: over 600,000 service files, ranging from 10 to 100 pages each, containing attestation papers, official forms and letters, financial statements and service records, medical reports and discharge records. On the afternoon of August 8, 2018, LAC finished the task. (I suspect the descendants of Private Joseph Zyvitski, Reg. No. 3320218, were ecstatic. The files were digitized alphabetically.)

Digitization is marvelous. But it is not magic. More than 40 people at Library and Archives Canada worked *full time* for four years to digitize the 622,290 Canadian Expeditionary Force files. LAC has estimated it would have taken one person 163 years to do the job. Before they could scan the documents, staff had to sort and clean the contents of each file, unfolding papers, repairing torn sheets, and removing adhesive tape, staples, and pins. In total, they extracted more than 570 pounds of metal, equivalent to a full-grown donkey.

Staff also had to provide descriptive information about the archives before digitization was complete. What is the point of digitizing a document or a photograph without providing any explanation of what it is? The archivists must also figure out how to store the digital content safely for as long as possible, and when and how to migrate the digital files from one piece of software to another when the computer technology changes, as it always does. Digitizing archives is more than a lifetime commitment. If the goal is to preserve something permanently, the processes used must endure well beyond the career of any individual archivist. Forever is a very, very long time.[3]

In the end, the final digitized collection of 30 million scanned images of personnel records occupies over 540 terabytes of computer space. If we wanted to transmit digital copies of all those service files from the Hubble telescope back to Earth, at 910 gigabytes a year, it would take 593 years. Nearly six centuries. Just for one collection, among the thousands of collections held in one archival institution in one country. The effort to digitize is not easy, fast, or cheap. By way of example, if NARA were to digitize each of the 25 million photographs in its collection, at a cost of $10.00 per image (an average estimate, according to digitization professionals), the total cost would be $250 million. That's two-thirds of NARA's *total* $400 million in annual expenditures for 2017. Imagine how much time, effort, and energy would be required to digitize everything, everywhere. I know people want that. They ask me all the time—why don't you digitize everything? Because, I say, if it costs as much to digitize *one* collection as it does to administer an entire national archival operation, tough choices must be made. Sorry.[4]

Like anyone wanting to use archives to make connections, I am thrilled when copies of archival materials can be made more widely available. But I have seen the inside of enough archival storage vaults to know that not everything—not even the smallest portion of everything—can or will be digitized. It is folly to assume we can scan everything and store it in a gigantic, comprehensive, cloud-based documentary nirvana.

Proving Life

When I see my Great Uncle Frank's service record, I feel a sense of connection with my family's past. Like others interested in their family history, I crave the links that can be made when I can access documents like military service files, marriage licenses, or birth certificates. But these bureaucratic records are valuable for so much more. It was deeply important to Americans, for instance, that Barack Obama could prove that when his feet landed on Planet Earth, they landed in the United States. But the process of registering births was not formalized in the United States until 1900. Before then, handwritten records of a baby's birth were most often found in family Bibles or baptismal registers. In England, compulsory registration of birth began in the 1830s; in Australia, it started around the 1850s. The New Zealand government formalized the process in 1856, even though an Anglican minister, the Reverend John Churton, had urged the government as early as 1842 to establish an official registry. Otherwise, he feared, the country was at risk of moral breakdown.[5]

A birth certificate matters for more than becoming president or being saved from moral ruin. A birth certificate provides us with our legal identity. Without a birth certificate, a person may not be able to access health care, attend school, hold a job, get a passport, or receive a driver's license; he may not be able to own land or open a bank account. Without a birth certificate, a child can be forced into marriage, pressed into slavery, or conscripted into the military because she cannot prove her right to object. The concern is so grave that the United Nations has declared the registration of children "immediately after birth" as an essential human right. Since 2005, humanitarian agencies such as Plan International have worked with countries worldwide to register the births of more than 40 million children.[6]

Despite international declarations of intent, however, more than 100 countries have not implemented formal registration systems.[7] When they have, the challenge of managing the evidence often hinders success. In Papua New Guinea, the government requires that babies are registered, but there is only one registration facility in the country, serving seven million people spread across 460,000 km^2 on 600 islands. In Myanmar, registration is entirely paper based, and the only copies exist at the local medical office. The forms delivered to the national government are discarded after two years. In Indonesia, the government can refuse to register a child if the parents cannot produce a marriage certificate. One wonders why such a critical piece of evidence as a birth certificate should be contingent on another piece of evidence, a marriage certificate, that can be so intricately bound up in social and cultural norms.[8]

Searching for Missing Links

What happens if your identity is a mystery? From the early years of the 20th century, some 7,000 child migrants or "home children" were transported from Britain and from British colonies to Australia in what was called "out-of-home" care. Another 450,000 Australian-born, nonindigenous children were put into foster care or state-run institutions. Many children were removed because their parents were divorced or widowed, others because the mother was unmarried and faced social stigma if she raised the child on her own. Children moved from orphanages to children's homes to foster homes, experiencing an upbringing that was haphazard at best, abusive at worst. As adults, many of these "forgotten Australians" (a controversial term because it might or might not include all three groups: aboriginal, migrant, and Australian-born) suffered a sense of abandonment and isolation, losing not only language and culture but also the family connections that so many others took for granted.

In 2001, the Australian government published a report called *Lost Innocents: Righting the Record—Report on Child Migration*, followed by the *Forgotten Australians* report in 2004. Both reports called for a national apology, which was made by the prime minister in 2009. The reports also asked for some form of redress.[9] In 2010, the Australian government announced it would invest $26.5 million (US$18.5 million) in a variety of Find & Connect services. The first tranche of funds, $3 million (US$2 million), was made available in 2011 specifically to help former child migrants and other "forgotten" children access counseling services, locate family members, and trace their family history. Some of the funds were used to support the development of a Find & Connect web resource, coordinated by a group of historians, archivists, and social workers from the University of Melbourne and Australian Catholic University. The resource provides guidance about how to search for records or locate agencies that might hold sources of evidence.[10]

The web resource itself does not contain actual records because, as its developers note, such information is personal and confidential. People must go to the agencies that provided care to find out what evidence is available, which may be only a handful of documents: an admission slip, perhaps, or a discharge statement. As (under)stated on the Find & Connect website, "Past record keeping practices of Government departments and 'care' providers were primarily for administrative purposes rather than to keep an accurate record of all events. Unfortunately, the older records may be superficial, inaccurate, or incomplete, and leave many questions unanswered."[11]

Frank Golding, who grew up in the care of three foster mothers and three different institutions, including the Ballarat Orphanage west of Melbourne, has worked closely with archivists in Australia to improve access to evidence. Children like him, he explains, were on the margins of society. They were "never given the opportunity to contribute to our personal record—so what passes as an account of our childhood is one-dimensional. . . . The makers of records could write opinions masquerading as facts without being made accountable for their value judgements."[12]

What is it like to know that a government office or private agency has evidence of your childhood but you are not allowed to see it because the caregivers involved were not your blood relatives? That you are part of a bureaucracy, not a family? Imagine receiving documents and seeing crucial information about you blacked out to protect the privacy of someone you might have called father or brother or mother. What kind of fragile connection is that?

Breaking Chains

What if you want to connect with your past but you are not descended from well-documented, mainstream folk? Or you can't even make a documentary connection to an orphanage or mission school? What if your ancestors were considered property, not people?

Barracoon: The Story of the Last "Black Cargo," by cultural anthropologist Zora Neale Hurston, recounts her interviews in 1927 with a man named Cudjo Lewis, originally known as Kossula, who was reported to be the last survivor of the last slave ship to arrive in the Americas. In the introduction to the book, Hurston explains how she first met with Cudjo, calling him by his African name, which made him bow his head with "tears of joy." When she told Cudjo that she wanted to know all about him, including "how you came to be a slave; and to what part of Africa do you belong, and how you fared as a slave, and how you have managed as a free man," he bowed his head again. When he lifted his face, he murmured,

> Thankee Jesus! Somebody come ast about Cudjo! I want tellee somebody who I is, so maybe dey go in de Afficky soil some day and callee my name and somebody dere say, 'Yeah, I know Kossula.' I want you everywhere you go to tell everybody whut Cudjo say, and how come I in Americky soil since de 1859 and never see my people no mo'.[13]

Between 1525 and 1866, more than 12 million Africans like Cudjo were enslaved and sent to North America, South America, and the Caribbean. The overwhelming majority of the 40 million African Americans living in the United States today are direct descendants of people whose identities and connections were taken from them without their permission. To help people search for their ancestors, Emory University in Atlanta, Georgia, hosts the Trans-Atlantic Slave Trade Database, which holds data about more than 35,000 individual slaving expeditions between 1514 and 1866, representing some 80 percent of African American slave trade activity. Included in the database are the names of ships, nations of origin, destinations, names of ship owners and captains, how many people were transported, and so on.[14]

The project team scoured archives and published sources from around the world to identify any reference to a slave ship, confirm the authenticity of the evidence, and transcribe the data into the database. Double- and triple-checking of data was essential to ensure the source evidence was replicated as accurately as possible. The database is a secondary source, though. The original evidence remains in archival collections around the world: ships' logs, letters to families, newspaper accounts, government reports, and personal diaries. If these archival institutions survive, the records they hold will continue to be preserved. But there is no guarantee that these unique sources of proof will remain intact and secure without constant care.[15]

When I search the Trans-Atlantic Slave Trade Database, I see that among the entries is a Chris Millar, who was captain of the *Fortune* in 1755, and an Alexander Millar, who was captain of the *King George* in 1807. Were these men my ancestors? I never connected my family with slavery. We were New Englanders and Loyalists. We had nothing to do with the American Civil War. Or did we?

Falling through the Cracks

It is one thing to seek connections with ancestors two centuries ago. What if your sense of identity and connection is challenged by the government of the day? How do people prove their citizenship, claim their property, or maintain their rights if a bureaucrat demands a piece of proof that never existed in the first place?

On June 22, 1948, hundreds of migrants from Jamaica arrived in London, England, on *MV Empire Windrush*. That year, the British government passed a law giving citizens of British colonies the right to settle in the United Kingdom, leading to an influx of immigrants from colonies around the world. Thousands of Caribbean immigrants, referred to as the "Windrush generation" after that first boatload from Jamaica, found new homes in England. At the time of their arrival, these migrants did not need to present passports or other documents on arrival. They were British citizens by law, which meant that the primary evidence associated with their arrival was not a stamped passport or a visa but a simple landing card or their names on a passenger list from the ship that brought them to England.

The difficulty arose in 2018, when the British government was accused of denying Caribbean migrants their rights as citizens. Some people who had arrived as part of the Windrush generation were threatened with deportation or with the loss of medical benefits or access to social services. To maintain their rights, these people were told they had to produce a stamped passport or visa to prove that they had entered the country legally 60 or 70 years earlier. Many people had no such proof. Others could access landing cards or passenger lists, including those in the National Archives, but the government had already destroyed some of those documents, believing they were no longer needed.[16]

Defining citizenship requirements for future generations is one question. Redefining them retroactively is quite another, especially if people are required to provide proof that never existed in the first place. Recordkeepers help identify the records that ought to be kept permanently; sometimes we face the impossible challenge of second-guessing what might be needed as evidence not just today but decades or centuries from now.[17]

Missing Evidence and Losing Rights

It is hard enough to defend your rights and protect your identity when you have some source of evidence. What happens when you have nothing? According to the United Nations' High Commissioner for Refugees, there are more than 25 million refugees around the world today, greater than half of them under the age of 18. Every day, 44,400 people escape their homes as a result of conflict or persecution.[18] They might have left their country with passports or birth certificates, but they may have lost the evidence along the way: stolen by smugglers; tossed overboard in their bags or backpacks to save weight on a raft; or damaged beyond repair as people moved from camp to camp. Refugees need sources of proof not just to maintain their identity and family connections but also to ensure their rights are protected.

The 1951 *United Nations Refugee Convention* and the 1967 *Protocol Relating to the Status of Refugees* outline the mechanisms protecting refugees around the world, including provisions for documenting a person's identity. According to article 27 of the *Convention*, Contracting States (the countries that ratified the convention) must issue identity papers to any refugee in their territory who does not arrive with a valid travel document.[19] Without evidence, a refugee may not be able to prove his educational achievements or professional qualifications. She may not be able to demonstrate her marital status or parental rights. He may not be able to verify his medical condition or health requirements, or confirm his right to money, possessions, or property in his home country.

A major recordkeeping responsibility today is to ensure that people arriving in a new country as refugees or asylum seekers have the documentary evidence they need to make a new life. This means not only creating valid sources of evidence on the spot but also respecting the different cultural norms associated with recordkeeping. For example, a couple might have been married according to the customs of their country, which may not have resulted in a written certificate. Will their marriage be considered legal in another country without a piece of paper as proof? Similarly, some religions prohibit a woman from exposing her face in public. How can she obtain identity papers without showing her face if she needs to get her photograph taken? These cross-cultural problems must be addressed effectively to ensure that sources of evidence serve as tools for resolution, not sources of conflict.

From Egypt in the second century to North America in the 21st, we are all connected. We are not the only people in the world, and our time is not the only time. There are many sides to any story. My father, a psychiatrist, used to warn me of the dangers of "temporal chauvinism": the belief that our moment is the best and only, and that no other time or place is worth acknowledging.

My mother, a jazz singer, was blunter, simply saying to me whenever I acted like a know-it-all, "Listen, Missy; a lot of things happened before you were born." A lot of things happened before any of us were born. Evidence helps us look beyond our own narrow world.

A legal principle, expressed in the Latin phrase *audi alteram partem*, says, "Let the other side be heard as well." No person should be judged without a fair hearing. This principle can be applied more broadly. Everyone in society should listen—*audi*—with an open mind in order to appreciate perspectives other than their own. Evidence helps us see the truth behind all sides of the story, not just the parts we want to see. Everyone has the right to know who they are and where they came from, even if the story is not a happy one. Evidence helps us make those connections, linking us not only to our immediate family but also to the rest of our kin on Planet Earth. Evidence helps keep us human *and* humane.

NOTES

1. Polion's letter was translated and analyzed by Grant Adamson, a graduate student in religious studies at Rice University. Adamson's report, "Letter from a Soldier in Pannonia," is published in *The Bulletin of the American Society for Papyrologists* 49 (2012): 79–94, https://cpb-us-e1.wpmucdn.com/news-network.rice.edu/dist/c/2/files/2014/03/2014-03-14-AdamsonPaper.pdf, *archived at* https://perma.cc/5MBF-J753. Rice University published the story online; see David Ruth, "Rice Grad Student Deciphers 1,800-Year-Old Letter from Egyptian Soldier," *Rice News*, March 14, 2014, http://news.rice.edu/2014/03/14/rice-grad-student-deciphers-1800-year-old-letter-from-egyptian-soldier, *archived at* https://perma.cc/2VY9-X5TY.

2. Information about Ancestry's holdings and operations changes regularly; the "Overview" page on the corporate website provides ever-changing statistics; see https://www.ancestry.ca/cs/legal/Overview, *archived at* https://perma.cc/Y2MR-X3PE.

3. Information about the Canadian Expeditionary Force digitization project can be found as part of LAC's Personnel Records of the First World War collection; see http://www.bac-lac.gc.ca/eng/discover/military-heritage/first-world-war/personnel-records/Pages/personnel-records.aspx, *archived at* https://perma.cc/VT4T-L5B4. More information about the project can also be found in the Fall/Winter 2017 issue of LAC's *Signatures* magazine at https://www.bac-lac.gc.ca/eng/about-us/publications/signatures/Pages/Signatures-2017-fall-winter.aspx, *archived at* https://perma.cc/7RPF-5KJF. See also the update on the LAC blog at https://thediscoverblog.com/2018/08/15/the-canadian-expeditionary-force-digitization-project-is-complete, *archived at* https://perma.cc/P697-GPXZ.

4. The UK-based Chartered Institute of Library and Information Professionals (CILIP) has estimated that it costs from 40 to 50 cents per page to digitize "normal" paper documents and from $4.00 to $17.00 per image to digitize photographs. The

report's author, Nick Poole, the Chief Executive of CILIP, estimated that the costs of digitizing all the holdings of The National Archives in the United Kingdom would be close to $50 billion. (All numbers, originally in Euro, have been converted to US dollars.) Poole's November 2010 report, *The Cost of Digitising Europe's Cultural Heritage: A Report for the Comité des Sages of the European Commission*, is available online at http://nickpoole.org.uk/wp-content/uploads/2011/12/digiti_report.pdf, *archived at* https://perma.cc/G3UR-PTCH. For budget information about NARA, see *National Archives FY 2018 Congressional Justification* (May 23, 2017), https://www.archives.gov/files/about/plans-reports/performance-budget/fy-2018-performance-budget.pdf, *archived at* https://perma.cc/M892-W6FJ.

5. See the Archives New Zealand descriptive entry at https://www.archway.archives.govt.nz/ViewFullItem.do?code=24749531, *archived at* https://perma.cc/H4DX-VXP9. A digital image of the letter is available at https://www.flickr.com/photos/archivesnz/26737234826, *archived at* https://perma.cc/E72T-9MU5. Interestingly, the Romans had established a process for registering births as early as 27 BC. In archival repositories around the world scholars have located some 21 birth registration documents for Roman citizens. Since our soldier friend Aurelius Polion seems to have been Egyptian (even though he served with the Roman army), it is unlikely that any of the 21 records relates to him. For a discussion of Roman birth recording processes, see Fritz Shulz, "Roman Registers of Births and Birth Certificates," *Journal of Roman Studies* 32, no. 1–2 (November 1942): 78–91.

6. For an interesting account of the importance of a birth certificate, see Christine Ro, "A Birth Certificate Is a Person's First Possession," *The Atlantic*, December 10, 2017, https://www.theatlantic.com/technology/archive/2017/12/a-birth-certificate-is-a-persons-first-possession/547970, *archived at* https://perma.cc/6WF2-RKP7. Also valuable is H. L. Brumberg, D. Dozor, and S. G. Golombek, "History of the Birth Certificate: From Inception to the Future of Electronic Data," *Journal of Perinatology* 32 (2012): 407–11, https://www.nature.com/articles/jp20123, *archived at* https://perma.cc/QFX5-RZ8U. See also United Nations Office of the Commissioner of Human Rights, *Convention on the Rights of the Child*, https://www.ohchr.org/en/professionalinterest/pages/crc.aspx, *archived at* https://perma.cc/LCP8-7AJL. Plan International's summary of its role in the birth registration process is available online; see Plan International, "Birth Registration," https://plan-international.org/early-childhood/birth-registration, *archived at* https://perma.cc/978Q-LWVA.

7. See Plan International, "Birth Registration."

8. United Nations Children's Fund, *Every Child's Birth Right: Inequities and Trends in Birth Registration* (UNICEF, 2013), https://www.un.org/ruleoflaw/files/Embargoed_11_Dec_Birth_Registration_report_low_res.pdf, *archived at* https://perma.cc/D9CT-8NPL.

9. The *Lost Innocents* report can be seen online at the Parliament of Australia website at https://www.aph.gov.au/Parliamentary_Business/Committees/Senate/Community_Affairs/completed_inquiries/1999-02/child_migrat/report/index.htm, *archived at* https://perma.cc/M6QN-NCFP. The *Forgotten Australians* report can be seen at https://www.aph.gov.au/Parliamentary_Business/Committees/Senate/Community_Affairs/Completed_inquiries/2004-07/inst_care/report/

index, *archived at* https://perma.cc/3ASK-RN3B. A follow-up report, *Lost Innocents and Forgotten Australians Revisited: Report on the Progress with the Implementation of the Recommendations of the Lost Innocents and Forgotten Australians Reports*, prepared in 2009, is available at https://www.aph.gov.au/Parliamentary_Business/ Committees/Senate/Community_Affairs/Completed_inquiries/2008-10/recs_lost _innocents_forgotten_aust_rpts/report/index, *archived at* https://perma.cc/T85C -MMPP.

10. The Find & Connect website is available at https://www.findandconnect.gov.au, *archived at* https://perma.cc/EH8X-Y9N5. Information specifically about funding is available at https://www.findandconnect.gov.au/about/background, *archived at* https://perma.cc/AG7L-UTXP. The British government also set up a £1 million (US$1.3 million) travel fund to allow former child migrants to visit families in the United Kingdom, which was later supplemented by the Australian government. Various Australian states developed schemes to provide financial compensation, but individuals wishing to receive funds had to present legal evidence of their claims, a requirement that proved problematic for many.

11. See Find & Connect, "What to Expect When Accessing Records about You," https:// www.findandconnect.gov.au/resources/what-to-expect-when-accessing-records, *archived at* https://perma.cc/XN39-9TZ3.

12. Frank Golding, "The Care Leaver's Perspective," *Archives and Manuscripts* 44, no. 3 (2016), 161. Work is also under way in England to understand more fully what happened to children who were put into state-run or private care facilities. The MIRRA (Memory–Identity–Rights in Records–Access) project, based at University College London, England, explores how child social care records were created, kept, and used. The project seeks input from care leavers themselves as well as from social workers and care professionals, archivists and information profession- als, and academic researchers. The goal is to identify ways to make such sensitive personal records more accessible in the future. For information on MIRRA, see the project website at https://blogs.ucl.ac.uk/mirra/sample-page, *archived at* https:// perma.cc/4B6M-HQTM.

13. Zora Neale Hurston, *Barracoon: The Story of the Last "Black Cargo"* (New York: Amistad, 2018), 19. Hurston, who had trained under the world-renowned anthro- pologist Franz Boas, chose to present Cudjo's words as authentically as possible, using his own dialect. Several publishers rejected the work, however, claiming the dialect was too difficult to follow. After multiple rejections, Hurston set the man- uscript aside and carried on with her life, publishing many other works, including poetry, essays, and novels. It took nearly 90 years for her account of Cudjo's expe- riences to be published.

14. For information about the database, see the official website for the Trans-Atlantic Slave Trade Database project at https://www.slavevoyages.org, *archived at* https:// perma.cc/5K4F-L7YQ. One of the resources in the database is a collection of the African names of slaves, whenever they could be found in archival sources. See https://www.slavevoyages.org/resources/names-database, *archived at* https:// perma.cc/DT6W-PJ8A.

15. For information on the history and methodology of the project, see https://www.slavevoyages.org/about/about, *archived at* https://perma.cc/494K-QFML. A comparable project is the Race and Slavery Petitions Project, at the University of North Carolina at Greensboro, which includes a searchable database of personal information about slaves, slaveholders, and free people of color, information that has been compiled by scouring the content of archival documents such as court petitions and other legal records from the fifteen slaveholding states between 1775 and 1867. For more information, see https://library.uncg.edu/slavery/petitions, *archived at* https://perma.cc/HT7L-U3AU.

16. See "Windrush Generation: Theresa May Apologises to Caribbean Leaders," *BBC News*, April 17, 2018, https://www.bbc.co.uk/news/uk-politics-43792411, *archived at* https://perma.cc/86LL-3GCX, and the National Archives website at http://discovery.nationalarchives.gov.uk/details/r/C9152210, *archived at* https://perma.cc/HE5E-SNDQ. See also Hugh Muir, "Caribritish: Me, My Family and the Legacy of Windrush," *BBC News*, June 7, 2018, https://www.theguardian.com/uk-news/2018/jun/07/caribritish-me-my-family-and-the-legacy-of-windrush, *archived at* https://perma.cc/BR3B-976N, and the UK Parliament's report, "Windrush Generation Detention," June 29, 2018, https://publications.parliament.uk/pa/jt201719/jtselect/jtrights/1034/103402.htm, *archived at* https://perma.cc/4FCK-7TSP.

17. See Dora Vargha, "Windrush Scandal: A Historian on Why Destroying Archives Is Never a Good Idea," *The Conversation*, April 24, 2018, https://theconversation.com/windrush-scandal-a-historian-on-why-destroying-archives-is-never-a-good-idea-95481, *archived at* https://perma.cc/HX6R-46UJ, and Amelia Gentleman, "Home Office Destroyed Windrush Landing Cards, Says Ex-staffer," *The Guardian*, April 17, 2018, https://www.theguardian.com/uk-news/2018/apr/17/home-office-destroyed-windrush-landing-cards-says-ex-staffer, *archived at* https://perma.cc/8ANV-T9BK.

18. See United Nations High Commissioner for Refugees, "Figures at a Glance" (June 19, 2018), http://www.unhcr.org/figures-at-a-glance.html, *archived at* https://perma.cc/33LX-XF4F.

19. For details, see the website for the United Nations High Commissioner for Refugees (UNHCR), esp. *Convention and Protocol Relating to the Status of Refugees* (Geneva: UNHCR, 2010), https://www.unhcr.org/3b66c2aa10, *archived at* https://perma.cc/5DVH-GN7W. A valuable initiative investigating the relationship between records and refugee rights included a symposium held in Budapest, Hungary, on January 10, 2018; information about the initiative can be found on the Open Society Archives website at http://www.osaarchivum.org/press-room/announcements/Symposium-Refugee-Rights-Records, *archived at* https://perma.cc/2B9A-4F6J, and also on the website for the Refugee Rights in Records Project, led by Anne Gilliland of UCLA and James Lowry of Liverpool University; see the project website at https://informationasevidence.org/refugee-rights-in-records, *archived at* https://perma.cc/5PP7-2BVH. For a discussion of the UNHCR and accountability, see *UNHCR and the Struggle for Accountability: Technology, Law and Results-Based Management*, ed. Kristin Bergtora Sandvik and Katja Lindskov Jacobsen (New York: Routledge, 2016).

6

"The secrecy helped spread the disease"

Evidence, Justice, and Rights

The records are crucial to hold us accountable. They are indispensable as deterrents against a repetition of this ghastliness and they are a powerful incentive for us to say, "Never again." They are a potent bulwark against human rights violations.
Archbishop Desmond Tutu, 2003

IT IS HEARTBREAKING TO LOOK AT THE PHOTOGRAPH OF THE THREE-year-old Syrian refugee Alan Kurdi, lying dead on a beach near Bodrum, Turkey. Only hours before the picture was taken, on September 3, 2015, Alan's parents had lifted him and his five-year-old brother into an inflatable boat, hoping to reach safety in Greece. A wave capsized the boat minutes after they pushed off, and Alan drowned, along with his mother and brother. When Turkish photojournalist Nilfur Demir of the Dogan News Agency saw Alan's body on the shore, she realized that "there was nothing left to do for him . . . nothing left to bring him back to life." So, she took her iconic photograph, thinking, "This is the only way I can express the scream of his silent body."[1]

The *Universal Declaration of Human Rights,* adopted by the United Nations in 1948, confirms that all people have the right to freedom, equality, identity, nationality, education, health, property, security, and privacy.[2] If the Syrian government and its military opponents had respected the 1948 declaration, perhaps Alan Kurdi's family would not have had to flee, and he would still be alive. But he is not. The photograph cannot bring Alan back to life, but it can serve as proof of the injustices his family endured, allowing us to defend the rights of others like him. No one can deny the truth of his death when they see this tragic piece of evidence.

In an ideal world, everyone would have access to authentic birth certificates, trustworthy property records, and other reliable sources of proof. Everyone would be able to access the evidence they need whenever they need it, from school records to pension statements to confirmation of health benefits. Government officials would create authentic and reliable records of their actions, and if those actions were discriminatory or dishonest, the public would be able to turn to evidence to demonstrate the injustice and seek redress. No one would need to leak evidence to the media because those in positions of power would use that power responsibly and would document their actions and decisions accurately. Everyone from politicians to schoolchildren would value recorded evidence not just as a source of history but as a foundation for democracy.

We do not live in that world. We live in the real world. In this real world, politicians are not always honest, bureaucrats make mistakes, and citizens can be denied their rights. In the real world, we need trustworthy evidence even more, as a witness to wrongs and as a tool for promoting justice and fighting for rights.

Seeking Justice in the Field

On April 15, 1989, in the worst disaster in British sporting history, 96 people died and another 766 were injured at the Hillsborough Football Stadium in Sheffield, England, when they were crushed against fences designed to hold football fans in "pens" during a semifinal game of the Football Association's FA Challenge Cup. A March 1991 inquest resulted in verdicts of accidental death in all cases, but many families objected, saying that the tragedy could have been prevented. A second coroner's inquest in 2016 overturned the original verdicts and ruled that the deaths were unlawful. The inquest found that the actions of the police and the ambulance services had directly contributed to the loss of life.

In 2009, the UK government established the Hillsborough Independent Panel to review all evidence of the disaster. The goal was to support "maximum possible public disclosure of governmental and other agency documentation." Part of the panel's remit was to work with the Keeper of Public Records to identify options for "establishing an archive of Hillsborough documentation, including a catalogue of all central governmental and local public agency information and a commentary on any information withheld for the benefit of the families or on legal or other grounds." The government believed that the public should have full and unfettered access to the documentary evidence of the tragedy and aftermath. The resulting collection of digital evidence serves to bring together as much documentation as possible of the actions, decisions, and opinions of all the parties involved. By preserving and making available digital copies of core evidence, the government is trying to rebuild public trust in the wake of tragedy.[3]

In June 2017, six people involved with the disaster, including police officers, were charged with offenses including manslaughter by gross negligence, misconduct in public office, and perverting the course of justice. As of 2019, several of the charges had been dropped, owing to insufficient evidence. The trials of David Duckenfield, the police match commander at the FA Challenge Cup semifinal, and Graham Mackrell, the Sheffield Wednesday Football Club secretary at the time, ended on April 3, 2019, only days before the 30th anniversary of the tragedy. The jury found Mackrell guilty of a health and safety charge, but the jurors were discharged after "failing" to reach a verdict on David Duckenfield. The Crown Prosecution Service has indicated it plans to seek a retrial in the Duckenfield case.[4]

Ironically, but perhaps inevitably, the government closed public access to the Hillsborough Archive in 2018 in order to support the privacy rights of people facing trial. The government promises that access will be restored as soon as all court cases have ended. It is a fact that even if evidence is preserved, it might not always be open for use. But if the records exist, and are kept safe, the possibility remains that they will become available someday. Someday is better than never. Which is what happens when essential evidence is not even created in the first place.[5]

Demanding Accountability

Iceland, a country of 350,000 people on an island less than 40,000 square miles around (95 times smaller than the United States), fell victim to the worldwide financial crisis of 2007–2008, when all three of Iceland's major banks (Kaupthing, Landsbanki, and Glitnir) collapsed in the same week in October 2008. Thousands of people lost homes and jobs. The Icelandic currency, the króna, weakened, and inflation rose to between 20 and 25 percent. The International Monetary Fund granted Iceland an emergency loan in November 2008 to help bridge the crisis. It was the greatest economic collapse in Iceland's history.

Outraged, the Icelandic public demanded that the government resign and the directors of the Central Bank be replaced. The "Pots and Pans Revolution," so called because people would gather in public spaces banging pots and pans as they protested, led to the fall of the government in January 2009. Bank managers were prosecuted, and many were found guilty of fraud, breach of trust, and insider trading.

In December 2008, the Icelandic Parliament established a Special Investigation Commission to determine why the banks had collapsed.[6] The commission was given wide authority to collect information: no one could refuse to answer the commission's questions. In April 2010, the commission released a 3,000-page report, which found that government agencies, including cabinet offices, exhibited serious weaknesses in recordkeeping and the management of information. For instance, formal minutes were not produced after government meetings. People would talk about issues but not create written summaries. According to Prime Minister Geir Haarde, the government's recordkeeping system was "primitive and outdated" ("frumstætt og gamaldags"). In 2018, Iceland's National Archivist Eiríkur Guðmundsson noted that rules were subsequently put in place to require the creation of core evidence and the registration of government communications, specifically to address recordkeeping weaknesses. Justice turns on the existence of documentary proof, and in this case, the government accepted its responsibility to strengthen the mechanisms for creating and protecting evidence. The documentary gaps are being closed.[7]

Uncovering a Dirty War

Yet another example of the importance of evidence for justice emerged in 2005, when a vast collection of documents belonging to the Guatemalan National Police was discovered in an abandoned warehouse in Guatemala City. Nearly 80 million sheets of paper (some five miles of records) were recovered, along with undeveloped films, videotapes, photographs, computer disks, and even vehicle license plates. The records prove that over 200,000 people had been abducted or killed, among them "non-combatants": innocent men, women, children, and religious and indigenous leaders. The evidence linked the Guatemalan National Police directly with the crimes.

In 1994, long before the documents were discovered, the government had established a Commission for Historical Clarification (La Comisión para el Esclarecimiento Histórico) to seek objective and impartial evidence of the events of the civil war, including the disappearance or death of hundreds of thousands of citizens. Despite the vision that the commission would clarify but not judge, however, the government resisted requests to share evidence. Officials claimed that records had been lost or destroyed or had never existed in the first place. The discovery of the police records in 2005 changed that conversation completely.

The records were in dreadful physical condition. Preserving them required armies of archival specialists, who reviewed, organized, and cleaned the records, prepared descriptions of the materials, digitized files, and stored the materials so that they were safe and accessible. These records might not have survived at all if archivists had not taken control. Because news of the cache of records became public, the Guatemalan government could not simply destroy the evidence, and because archival experts applied their technical and professional expertise, the records can stand as reliable evidence, not jumbled and confused piles of paper. Today, the records, now known as the Historical Archive of the National Police (AHPN), may represent the most extensive collection of "dirty war" documentation ever found in Latin America.[8]

Unfortunately, the archives are still not secure. In August 2018, the Guatemalan government removed the director of the Historical Archive of the National Police from his position, replacing him with an inexperienced bureaucrat. The government also ended the independence of the archives by giving the local United Nations Development Programme (UNDP) office, in collaboration with the Ministry of Culture, direct oversight of operations. The government also put the remaining 52 archives staff members on temporary contract, imperiling the sustainability of the operation. Neither the government nor the United Nations has offered any explanation for these unprecedented changes. If evidence is going to be used to defend rights and protect justice, then perpetual and impartial oversight is essential. In this case, external management by neutral agents has been replaced by direct control by potentially biased players. Such decisions can turn valuable archival collections into secret hoards.[9]

Exposing a Circle of Secrecy

More secrets emerged in Pennsylvania in August 2018, when the state's attorney general announced the release of what he called the "largest, most comprehensive report into child sexual abuse within the Catholic Church ever produced in the United States." The report, written over two years by 23 grand jurors, outlines in shattering detail the abuse of victims by clergy in six Catholic dioceses across the state, in 54 of Pennsylvania's 67 counties.[10]

The grand jury heard testimony from dozens of witnesses, reviewed half a million pages of internal diocesan documents, located proof of allegations against over 300 priests, and identified more than 1,000 child victims. As the jury members noted, the church's methods were a "playbook for concealing the truth." It was discovered that reports issued by church officials to law enforcement agencies were too general to serve as verifiable evidence: the statements in them would likely not stand up to legal scrutiny. As well, proof of wrongdoing had been left out of police reports. Documentary evidence was in plain sight in the church's own records, but those records were kept hidden from anyone outside a small circle of church insiders. "The main thing," the jury wrote, "was not to help children, but to avoid 'scandal.'" "Scandal," the jury added, is not our word, but theirs; it appears over and over again in the documents we recovered. Abuse complaints were kept locked up in a "secret archive." That is not our word, but theirs; the church's Code of Canon Law specifically requires the diocese to maintain such an archive. Only the bishop can have the key.[11]

Bishop Wuerl of Pittsburgh (later Cardinal of Washington, DC) said that the church operated a "circle of secrecy." As the jury confirmed, "The bishops weren't just aware of what was going on; they were immersed in it. And they went to great lengths to keep it secret. The secrecy helped spread the disease."[12] Shortly after the report was released, Pope Francis issued a letter acknowledging that "the heart-wrenching pain of these victims, which cries out to heaven, was long ignored, kept quiet or silenced." Silenced indeed. In this case, evidence existed that could have stopped the abuse and opened the door to justice. But it was intentionally suppressed in a "secret archive." Preserving evidence is not enough if that evidence is never made available.[13]

Carving a Path

To ensure we live in a society that upholds justice and defends human rights, everyone in that society needs to fight the suppression of proof. But we must also remember that our definition of proof may not be the same as someone else's. If evidence is a social construct and if every society defines evidence its own way, what happens when two societies need to come to some sort of agreement but they do not share the same interpretation of evidence? What happens when I am satisfied with a handshake and you demand a written agreement? Who gets justice, and whose voice remains silent? Protecting rights for all means broadening our perception of evidence.

In Canada, 1.6 million of Canada's 36 million people identify as indigenous (First Nations, Métis, and Inuit). After Europeans first came to Canada in the 1600s, bringing their own legal and social systems, indigenous and nonindigenous people began a struggle, which continues to this day, as different understandings of ownership and rights came into sharp conflict. Acknowledging that I can only skate over centuries of history here, let me say that by the 20th century, the dominant governance systems across Canada were almost entirely based on British and French norms. Indigenous concepts of law, justice, property ownership, and rights were subordinated or ignored. In some parts of the country written treaties were signed and upheld; in other parts treaties were incomplete or ignored; and in other parts of the country, no agreement was ever reached. Conflicting claims over land, resource management, and other rights persist to this day.[14]

One of the enduring struggles is that Western and indigenous concepts of evidence were and are very different. In Eurocentric systems, direct witness testimony has long been the favored form of admissible evidence in a court of law. If I saw something happen, I could swear an oath that I was telling the truth. My oral statement would be duly considered by judge and jury. Documents could be admitted only if their authenticity could be demonstrated. Were they part of a structured recordkeeping system? Could they be proven to be authentic, unchanged, and complete?

In this Western system, hearsay testimony—a statement from someone who cannot claim to have been an eyewitness to the events in question—is not normally considered acceptable evidence. Oral histories, while perceived as a valuable contribution to historical collections, were not normally seen as "pure" evidence, comparable to direct witness testimony, or even to a document, if its provenance and chain of custody can be authenticated. But in indigenous communities, oral histories were and are a valued form of evidence. Traditionally passed down from person to person according to prescribed rituals, they convey family or community histories in detail. Indigenous groups also document tribal responsibilities on totem poles, create beaded belts to record financial transactions, etch animal skins with images documenting events over the year, and share facts and ideas through songs and stories.[15] Despite the richness of indigenous forms of evidence, though, they have rarely been accepted in Western law.

As indigenous communities came into conflict over land rights in Canada, they brought their evidence forward for consideration, but the Eurocentric approach dominated. Conflicts arose particularly in the 1980s and 1990s as indigenous groups protested provincial and federal government decisions about land rights, fishing, hunting, and resource extraction. Finally, a fundamental change came in 1997, when British Columbia Justice C. J. Lamar made a short but highly significant legal declaration. Evidence, he acknowledged, could not be defined by only its form. "Notwithstanding the challenges created by the use of oral histories as proof of historical facts," he stated, "the laws of evidence must be adapted in order that this type of evidence can be accommodated and placed on an equal footing with the types of historical evidence that courts are familiar with, which largely consists of historical documents."[16]

Lamar's words helped to point Canadians in a new direction, encouraging a more wide-ranging interpretation of evidence. Today, even though people on both "sides" perceive the success of this effort differently, much has changed.

Small steps are being taken to pursue greater mutual understanding and respect.

Seeking Reconciliation

This reinterpretation of evidence became important on June 11, 2008, when Canadian Prime Minister Stephen Harper issued an apology to indigenous communities across the country on behalf of the Canadian government and all federal political parties, for the role of past governments in administering "Indian Residential Schools," or IRSs. The 80 or so church-run schools across Canada had housed more than 86,000 indigenous children from the 1870s to 1996. The focus of these schools was on assimilation. Children were punished if they attempted to speak their own languages instead of English or French, and access to their families was limited or nonexistent. Many children were also subject to physical, sexual, and mental abuse at the hands of priests, teachers, and others. Later, many students developed addictions to alcohol and drugs, living destabilized, high-risk lives. Suicide rates among former students remain high today, and medical studies have shown that the trauma can be passed down to children and grandchildren.

As part of its apology, the government committed to the establishment of a Truth and Reconciliation Commission, or TRC, to uncover the "truth" about the schools. As with any search for fact-based truth, the real search was for evidence. But this time, it was recognized that written evidence was not the only source of reliable proof. Oral histories and family recollections were also considered valuable sources. The question of subjectivity of memory was considered less crucial than the importance of allowing people the opportunity to express their personal truths. The TRC traveled the country gathering witness statements, identifying sources of documentary evidence in churches, schools, and government archives, and holding public and private meetings across the country to hear testimony from former students and their families.

In its final report, issued in 2015, the TRC included several recommendations specifically related to the management of evidence. A National Centre for Truth and Reconciliation (NCTR) was established in Winnipeg, Manitoba, to house the more than five million documentary records copied from archival repositories across the country.[17] Library and Archives Canada was urged to adopt and implement the *United Nations Declaration on the Rights of Indigenous Peoples*, which confirmed the right of indigenous people to use their own systems of recordkeeping and memory making, including oral traditions. The TRC also urged governments across the country to broaden their approach to archival service to incorporate indigenous ways of learning and knowing.[18]

Balancing Access with Privacy

Another part of the TRC settlement allowed former residential school students to make a claim against the government for sexual or physical abuse or other "wrongful acts." The Independent Assessment Process, or IAP, that accompanied the claim required applicants to attend a hearing, overseen by a neutral adjudicator, to testify about their experiences. Nearly 38,000 IAP applications were received as of early 2014, and over 20,000 separate hearings were held.[19]

A conflict then arose over whether to preserve the IAP records, which include graphic and emotional testimony, as archival evidence. Some believed the records provide valuable proof of abuse, while others believed they are too personal and ought to be destroyed after claims have been completed. In the end, the Supreme Court of Canada decided that privacy should take precedence over posterity. It ruled in 2017 that the government should retain the IAP records for 15 years, during which time individual claimants could confirm if they wanted their own IAP documents kept in the archives. After 15 years, if no other provision has been made to retain individual case files, they are to be destroyed.

This decision respects personal privacy. But it seems cruelly ironic. By documenting their recollections in written form, claimants have turned their personal and shared memories into Western-style evidence. If that written evidence is then destroyed, and if the claimants do not pass their stories on in another way—through traditional oral histories, perhaps—then their voices will eventually be silenced. What will remain in the archives might be the records of those in power, but not the evidence of those who suffered at their hands. Is that the right result, if the goal is reconciliation?[20]

Recognizing Stolen Generations

In 1995, the Australian government launched an inquiry similar to the Canadian Truth and Reconciliation Commission to investigate the relocation of Australian aboriginal and Torres Strait Islander children. Aboriginal and mixed-race children had been removed from their families and put into church missions to integrate them into white society. Government officials believed that the aboriginal population would inevitably become extinct, and they felt that relocating children was a necessary part of assimilation.

The 1995 study resulted in the *Report of the National Inquiry into the Separation of Aboriginal and Torres Strait Islander Children from Their Families* (known as the *Bringing Them Home* report), tabled in the Australian Parliament on May 26, 1997. The protection of evidence was a highlight of the report. Recommendation 21 required that no records should be destroyed if they related to children who had been removed from their families, and Recommendation 22 required that all government agencies be funded "as a matter of urgency" to preserve and make available relevant documentary evidence, while respecting personal privacy.[21]

The inquiry also recognized that many people found it difficult to access evidence about themselves, either because the files could not be found or because the different departments holding the records imposed different conditions on access. Some agencies levied fees, while others left people waiting a long time before granting access. Restrictions to "third-party" information might mean that the piece of information needed—the missing link—might be the very piece withheld from view.

Ensuring the evidence is preserved and made available is essential to supporting evidence-based truth about the past. Still, the experience of seeing the files can be terribly emotional. As one person said, "There are a lot of untrue things about me on those files. I have cried about the lies on those files."[22] One has to ask, though, if it is worse to search for justice and find nothing at all.

In the ideal world I long for, we would not have to fight so hard to protect evidence because we would not need to prove corruption or fight against misconduct or abuse. But we do not live in that world. If we are going to respect rights and uphold justice in the real world, we need authentic sources of proof. But evidence is both valuable and vulnerable. We all need to work together to protect it from the moment it is created, so that it is available when we need it, whether now or a century from now.

Documentary evidence cannot bring Alan Kurdi back to life. But Nilfur Demir's photograph will keep him alive in the hearts of those who struggle to defend human rights against all enemies. Her photograph should be heard as a scream—that law, justice, and human rights matter. That people matter.

NOTES

1. The story of Demir's photograph, which was named one of *Time*'s 100 most influential photographs of all time, can be found in various online sources, including on *Time*'s website at http://100photos.time.com/photos/nilufer-demir-alan-kurdi, *archived at* https://perma.cc/JH6U-ZLYJ, and in CNN reporter Brandon Grigg's story, "Photographer Describes 'Scream' of Migrant Boy's 'Silent Body,'" *CNN World*, September 3, 2015, https://edition.cnn.com/2015/09/03/world/dead-migrant-boy -beach-photographer-nilufer-demir, *archived at* https://perma.cc/7PH3-FU4R.

2. For the text of the *Universal Declaration of Human Rights*, see the United Nations website at www.un.org/en/universal-declaration-human-rights/index.html, *archived at* https://perma.cc/HK2F-DY9V.

3. See the terms of reference for the committee in appendix 1 of its official report, *Hillsborough: The Report of the Hillsborough Independent Panel* (London: The Stationery Office, September 2012), https://www.gov.uk/government/publications/the -report-of-the-hillsborough-independent-panel, *archived at* https://perma.cc/ 2JHM-7AB8, esp. 377 and 369. For an insider's perspective on the work of the Hillsborough Independent Panel, see Sarah Tyacke, "Trusting the Records: The Hillsborough Football Disaster 1989 and the Work of the Independent Panel 2010–12," in *Do Archives Have Value?*, ed. Michael Moss and David Thomas (London: Facet, forthcoming 2019).

4. See Joe Thomas, "Hillsborough Verdict Updates: Graham Mackrell Guilty but Jury Discharged Over David Duckenfield," *Liverpool Echo*, April 3, 2019, https://www .liverpoolecho.co.uk/news/liverpool-news/live-duckenfield-mackrell-hillsborough -trial-15673572, *archived at* https://perma.cc/3UWF-DCGD. Several events took place to mark the 30th anniversary, as outlined in "Liverpool Marks 30 Years since Hillsborough Disaster," *BBC News*, April 14, 2019, https://www.bbc.com/news/ uk-england-merseyside-47912890, *archived at* https://perma.cc/6SWQ-U9QG.

5. See Tyacke, "Trusting the Records." As of April 2019, the official website for the Hillsborough Archive was still not open to the public, pending the completion of legal proceedings. See https://webarchive.nationalarchives.gov.uk/*/http:// hillsborough.independent.gov.uk, *archived at* https://perma.cc/S5ES-LWHC.

6. Unlike in the United States, the Icelandic government did not consider providing bailouts to the banks. As argued by Gudrun Johnsen, a professor of finance at Reykjavik University and a senior researcher for the Special Investigation Commission, "There was a benefit in the entire system going down. We know what failed and as a consequence we were able to clean house pretty quickly." See "How Did Iceland Clean Up Its Banks?," *BBC News*, February 10, 2016, https://www.bbc.com/ news/business-35485876, *archived at* https://perma.cc/PE5L-422R.

7. There is another privacy wrinkle in the Icelandic story. In 2009, WikiLeaks disseminated internal documents from Kaupthing Bank. The leaks showed how the bank loaned money to various owners and wrote off large debts shortly before the collapse. The bank challenged WikiLeaks' right to publish the information but was rebuffed by WikiLeaks' legal counsel. See the correspondence between Kaupthing Bank and WikiLeaks' legal counsel at https://wikileaks.org/wiki/Icelandic_bank _Kaupthing_threat_to_WikiLeaks_over_confidential_large_exposure_report,_

31_Jul_2009, *archived at* https://perma.cc/EGH9-22YR. After Iceland's Special Investigation Commission ended its work, its own records—over 30 linear feet of paper files, more than 90 gigabytes of digital data, and 147 audio and video interviews—were transferred to the National Archives of Iceland, which then took on responsibility for preserving the evidence and providing access. Given the serious financial implications of the banking crisis (and, one assumes, the complications arising from the fact that some evidence had been leaked), the archives faced a David-and-Goliath battle against a range of international insurance companies that sought access to restricted information in the records. In the end, the Icelandic Supreme Court consistently ruled in the archives' favor. I am grateful to Eiríkur G. Guðmundsson, National Archivist of Iceland, for his various inputs via email in September 2018 as well as for making available a copy of his speech to the Association of Canadian Archivists, "Keeping the Truth" (June 6–9, 2018). See also the Special Investigation Commission's report, *Background and Causes of the Icelandic Banks' Collapse in 2008 and Related Events*, vol. 8 (Reykjavik: Althingi, 2010), 147, https://www.rna.is/media/skjol/RNABindi8.pdf, *archived at* https://perma.cc/ DY5D-U7JK. An English summary and excerpts from the report are available at https://www.rna.is/eldri-nefndir/addragandi-og-orsakir-falls-islensku-bankanna -2008/skyrsla-nefndarinnar/english, *archived at* https://perma.cc/BMJ7-LDL2. In perhaps unrelated news, the National Archives of Iceland announced in October 2018 that it had run out of storage space and was no longer receiving new transfers of government archives until storage issues had been resolved. See Jelena Ćirić, "No More Room at National Archives," *Iceland Review*, October 22, 2018, https:// www.icelandreview.com/news/room-national-archives, *archived at* https://perma .cc/7T7U-46F8.

8. Details about the records, and the context in which they were created, used, and found, can be found in the English translation of the Commission for Historical Clarification's *From Silence to Memory: Revelations of the Archivo Histórico de la Policía Nacional*, with a foreword by Carlos Aguirre and a preface by Kate Doyle, published by the University of Oregon Libraries in 2013 and available online at https:// scholarsbank.uoregon.edu, *archived at* https://perma.cc/4RLH-3XZG. The original Spanish version was published in 1999, before the archives were discovered. See also Kate Doyle's account, *The Guatemalan Police Archives* (National Security Archive Electronic Briefing Book No. 170), National Security Archive, November 21, 2005, https://nsarchive2.gwu.edu//NSAEBB/NSAEBB170/index.htm, *archived at* https:// perma.cc/T3KL-DU5C. See also Kirsten Weld, *Paper Cadavers: The Archives of Dictatorship in Guatemala* (Durham, NC: Duke University Press, 2014).

9. The news of this change in leadership was announced in a National Security Archive press release, "Guatemala Police Archive under Threat" (August 13, 2018), https:// nsarchive.gwu.edu/news/guatemala/2018-08-13/guatemala-police-archive-under -threat#.W3Q7pZokZwo.e-mail, *archived at* https://perma.cc/G8BT-W8RA. See also Aisling Walsh, "Impunity Reigns: Threats to the Historical Archive of the National Police in Guatemala," *DemocraciaAbierta*, September 2, 2018, https://www.open democracy.net/democraciaabierta/aisling-walsh/impunity-reigns-threats-to -historical-archive-of-national-police-in-, *archived at* https://perma.cc/8ENM-L6D2.

10. The report, *40th Statewide Investigating Grand Jury Report 1 Interim—Redacted*, is available online through various links, including within the CNN report by Daniel Burke, "Pennsylvania Sex Abuse Report Presents Crucial Test for Pope Francis," *CNN Religion*, August 17, 2018, https://www.cnn.com/2018/08/16/us/pennsylvania-catholic-church-vatican-response/index.html, *archived at* https://perma.cc/U4MF-AU2H.

11. See *Grand Jury Report*, 2–3.

12. Ibid., 300.

13. See Pope Francis, "Letter of His Holiness Pope Francis to the People of God," published as "In Full: Pope Francis' Letter on Child Sex Abuse and Cover-Ups," *BBC News*, August 20, 2018, https://www.bbc.co.uk/news/world-45250452, *archived at* https://perma.cc/59JE-YSTD.

14. There are so many books available on indigenous history in Canada that choosing one over another is impossible. As a starting point, I recommend Olive Patricia Dickason and William Newbigging, *A Concise History of Canada's First Nations* (Toronto: Oxford University Press, 2015).

15. I discuss the intersection between indigenous and nonindigenous recordkeeping traditions in "'Subject or Object?' Shaping and Reshaping the Intersections between Aboriginal and Non-Aboriginal Records," *Archival Science* 6, no. 3–4 (December 2006): 329–50. My analysis in that article was challenged by Aaron Gordon in his PhD dissertation, "Eurocentric Archival Knowledge Production and Decolonizing Archival Theory" (Toronto: York University, 2014). More recent works on indigenous archives include J. J. Ghaddar, "The Spectre in the Archive: Truth, Reconciliation, and Indigenous Archival Memory," *Archivaria* 82 (Fall 2016), and Krista McCracken, "Community Archival Practice: Indigenous Grassroots Collaboration at the Shingwauk Residential Schools Centre," *The American Archivist* 78, no. 1 (Spring/Summer 2015): 181–91.

16. See *Delgamuukw v. British Columbia*, File No. 23799, 1997: June 16, 17; 1997: December 11, https://scc-csc.lexum.com/scc-csc/scc-csc/en/item/1569/index.do?r=AAAAAQAtUi4gdi4gU3BhcnJvdyAoMTk5MCwgU3VwcmVtZSBDb3Vyd CBvZiBDYW5hZGEpAAAAAAAAAQ, *archived at* https://perma.cc/39SH-YU2Z.

17. See the information on the NCTR website at http://nctr.ca/about-pages.php#mandate, *archived at* https://perma.cc/3TS2-NBS4.

18. All TRC reports and associated documents are available on the official website for the National Centre for Truth and Reconciliation at http://nctr.ca/reports2.php, *archived at* https://perma.cc/S495-D6NB. Recommendation 70i is shown on page 258 of the final report, *Honouring the Truth, Reconciling for the Future* (Truth and Reconciliation Commission of Canada, 2015), at http://nctr.ca/assets/reports/Final%20Reports/Executive_Summary_English_Web.pdf, *archived at* https://perma.cc/4BFA-HBUP. Article 13 of the *United Nations Declaration on the Rights of Indigenous Peoples* (United Nations, 2008) addresses the right to languages, traditions, and literatures; see https://www.un.org/esa/socdev/unpfii/documents/DRIPS_en.pdf, *archived at* https://perma.cc/8HRR-UUYJ.

19. For information about the IAP, see the fact sheets at http://www.iap-pei.ca/ pub-eng.php?act=factsheets/irsas-pamplet-eng.php, *archived at* https://perma .cc/2QYV-YS4U.

20. The justices noted that it was not possible to consider the wishes of deceased claimants who might have wanted their records preserved, but they argued that "the destruction of records that some claimants would have preferred to have preserved works a lesser injustice than the disclosure of records that most expected never to be shared." The judgment itself, *Canada (Attorney General) v. Fontaine*, can be seen at https://scc-csc.lexum.com/scc-csc/scc-csc/en/item/16797/index.do, *archived at* https://perma.cc/55E4-KE7J. See also Kathleen Harris, "Indigenous Residential School Records Can Be Destroyed, Supreme Court Rules," *CBC News*, October 6, 2017, http://www.cbc.ca/news/politics/indian-residential-schools -records-supreme-court-1.4343259, *archived at* https://perma.cc/KU2C-Z9NY.

21. The *Bringing Them Home* report can be accessed via https://bth.humanrights.gov .au, *archived at* https://perma.cc/E8VN-4N2C.

22. See Human Rights and Equal Opportunity Commission, *A Community Guide to the Findings and Recommendations of the National Inquiry into the Separation of Aboriginal and Torres Strait Islander Children from Their Families* (updated December 2007), 9. This guide, which supports the interpretation and application of the *Bringing Them Home* report, is available at https://www.humanrights.gov.au/sites/default/ files/content/pdf/social_justice/bth_Community%20guide_final.pdf, *archived at* https://perma.cc/69XN-4UZ4. See chapter 16 of the *Bringing Them Home* report for a discussion of third-party access and privacy issues.

7

"A mysterious and malleable thing"

Evidence, Memory, and Narrative

One of the great things about history is that it sort of isn't a done deal—ever. The historical texts and the historical evidence that you use is always somehow giving you different answers because you're asking it different questions.

Mary Beard, 2016

ON NOVEMBER 22, 1963, I WAS PLAYING IN MY PARENTS' BEDROOM when the announcement came over the radio that President Kennedy had been shot in Dallas, Texas. My mother was changing my brother's diaper when she heard the news. I watched her collapse on the floor and burst into tears. I saw my brother lying on the bed, his diaper unpinned. Baby powder was spilling onto the bedspread. Frightened, I started to cry. My brother began to wail. The announcer murmured in the background as the bedroom exploded with grief.

Of course, when President Kennedy was shot, I was four years old. I don't think I actually *remember* anything. What I carry, I believe, are not personal memories but the imprint of family stories, repeated so often that I have incorporated them into my own consciousness. Like a Borg drone taking orders from the Queen in an episode of *Star Trek*, I have assimilated knowledge about my personal collective. I was there at the time, and I was there when the stories were told later. So now I "remember" it. Do I remember the truth? I don't know. Does it matter? I don't know. It is *my* truth.

If someone had taken a photograph of my mother, my brother, and me in that bedroom, or filmed us with a home movie camera, or captured our cries on audiotape, we would have proof. Recorded evidence helps build a collection of memories that define who we are and how we fit into our families, communities, and societies. Some things we may recall, and some are perhaps only echoes.

I don't remember being born, but I have a birth certificate that proves that when my feet landed on Planet Earth, they landed in Seattle, Washington. It must be true that I was born in Seattle. I don't remember knowing my grandfather, but I have a photograph of him holding my hand. It must be true that I knew him. I know I gave a speech on memory and archives in Vienna in 2004, though what I remember most is the amazing banquet, or at least the generous servings of Austrian wine. But in my personal archives is a copy of the speech, along with the program for the conference, and (relatively benign) photographs of me at the dinner. It must be true. I was there. I gave that speech. (And, I expect, I drank the wine.)

Evidence serves as a touchstone: a tangible link between our memories, which can be remarkably fragile, and provable facts, which are immutable. Evidence can be interpreted in official narratives, such as history books or newspaper stories, and then reinterpreted again and again to produce different conclusions. Evidence links personal memories with official stories, enriching our personal lives, helping us to define ourselves, and enhancing our understanding of others. It can also serve as a vitally important corrective, when what we think happened and what actually transpired are at odds. Evidence can save memories, and it can save lives.

Verifying Our Memories

I may not have a recording that substantiates my memory of Kennedy's assassination. But Abraham Zapruder did. On November 22, 1963, Zapruder, a 58-year-old Ukrainian-American dress manufacturer, slipped out of work for an hour to watch Kennedy and his entourage travel along the road in Zapruder's hometown of Dallas, Texas. Zapruder brought his Bell & Howell Zoomatic film camera with him, and as the motorcade started to pass, Zapruder turned on the machine. His film, running a mere 26.6 seconds, is considered the most complete moving image of the assassination. It is a pivotal piece of documentary evidence.

In 1992, 22 years after Zapruder's death, President George H. W. Bush declared the film an "official" assassination record, meaning it was now considered government property. Zapruder's family protested, demanding the return of the original film, which the government had taken into its possession mere hours after the assassination. In 1999, the government agreed to pay the family $16 million to buy the film, but through the wondrous wrinkles of copyright law, the family retained the intellectual property rights. The family donated copyright to the film to the Sixth Floor Museum in Dallas, Texas, which is dedicated to the life and death of President Kennedy.[1]

Zapruder's film has become an iconic archival symbol of the assassination. It is also a touchstone, bringing back memories for anyone alive in 1963. When I watch the film, I swear I can hear my mother's cries.

Remembering What We Forgot

It is wonderful to reconnect with your family's past. But what if you cannot remember it? Alzheimer's disease and other forms of dementia seem to me a kind of mental prison, without light or warmth. Neurologists and gerontologists have found, though, that people's long-term memories can be stimulated if they are exposed to sounds and images from the past. In 2016, with support from the British Alzheimer's Society, the BBC's Archive Development team worked with Dundee University and the University of St. Andrews to compile RemArc (Reminiscence Archive), a collection of digitized items from the BBC's archives. Included are some 1,500 digital clips of video, audio recordings, and photographs, dating from the 1930s to the 2000s, all copied from the BBC's archival holdings. The materials are organized by theme and decade: animals, people, childhood activities, or popular events in history. Images show everything from hot air balloon rides to ballroom dancing to skinheads. There is an audio recording of King George's Christmas speech in 1932, and a video clip of David Attenborough sitting with a gorilla in 1979. (The gorilla looks unimpressed.) One of the users of RemArc said, "I could sit here all day," and another said, "It makes you realize how much you thought you'd forgotten."[2] It is so rewarding to see someone's eyes shine when an archival image or sound helps to bring back a memory.

Restoring Family Ties

What if you have no memory? How can evidence help then? In the case of a small series of British Army films, the sound of a voice gave one woman a memory she never had as a child. In 1984, workers renovating Manchester's town hall found 40 reels of British Army films. The *Calling Blighty* series of short films, produced between 1944 and 1946, showed army personnel stationed in India, Burma, Malaya, and other locations in Southeast Asia greeting their families back home. Of the nearly 400 films produced, only 64 are known to survive, including the 40 found in the basement in Manchester.

Along with the canisters of film were documents listing the names and addresses of family and friends who had been contacted to attend the Manchester screenings during the war. In November 2015, the lists were used to contact relatives, along with two surviving veterans, who were invited to a screening and to participate in a Channel 4 documentary about the movies. Among the relatives at the screening was Ann Alsop. Her father, 31-year-old Corporal John Hartley of the Second Battalion East Lancashire Regiment, is shown in one of the films: "Issue Number 149." He is seen greeting his family back home in Manchester, sending his best wishes to Mildred, Mother, and Dad, then chirping, "Trust you are all well. I'm in the pink."

John died in Burma soon after the film was made, on August 27, 1944. His daughter never met him. She has no other evidence of his life. According to Ann, her mother, the Mildred whom John said hello to in the film, destroyed all his photos and letters and changed her daughter's name to that of her stepfather. After viewing the film, Ann travelled to Burma to visit John's grave and learn more about his death: shot, apparently, by a retreating Japanese sniper.[3]

I cannot imagine what it would be like to hear your father's voice for the very first time more than 70 years after his death. From 20 seconds of archival footage, Ann Alsop can create a memory where none existed before: the memory of a father she finally "met," decades after his death. My discovery of Great Uncle Frank pales in comparison.

Destroying Evidence

The thing about personal memories is that they are so personal. None of us is obligated to make, keep, or share our family photographs, love letters, or personal diaries. As I discuss later, public officials are legally bound to create and preserve some types of evidence, though the laws are often weak and poorly enforced. But in our domestic lives, we have every right not to leave any documentary traces. Archivists struggle with this reality. Why would anyone not want to be remembered? (Mind you, archivists get paid to read other people's mail. Is there a modicum of self-interest in our attachment to evidence?)

In September 1806, the British novelist Charles Dickens set fire to thousands of personal letters, upset, apparently, because some personal correspondence with a business associate had found its way into the press. American and British newspapers were reporting on his separation from his wife and speculating that he was having an affair with an English actress. He was, it seems, none too happy with his personal life making its way into public conversations.[4] I suspect that Dickens was embarrassed; he didn't want his secrets made public. But everyone's life is full of difficult, embarrassing, or sad memories. How can we learn from them, or allow others to learn from them, if we turn our backs on the proof?

Zora Neale Hurston, who wrote *Barracoon*, left instructions to burn her remaining property after her death, including her manuscripts, but when a friend of hers saw the fire, he put it out, saving many of her papers. They were later acquired by the University of Florida. Today, if you look at digital copies of her archives on the university library's website, you can see the burn marks along the edges of the documents.[5]

Dickens's and Hurston's archives provide examples not only of the impulse to erase the past but also of the destructive force of fire. From the time of the "great fire" at the Royal Library at Alexandria, in Egypt, archives have been lost not just to neglect but also to disaster. In 1940, a bomb fell on the British Museum, damaging hundreds of books in the King's Library. On July 12, 1973, a fire at the US National Personnel Records Center destroyed close to 18 million official military personnel files.[6] The California wildfires in 2017 destroyed not just entire neighborhoods but also vast quantities of documentary evidence, including the archives of the Hewlett-Packard Company, one of the oldest and largest technology companies in the world. The November 2018 Camp Fire in California, which the State of California declared the most destructive and deadliest wildfire in California's history, resulted in 88 deaths and the incineration of 13,972 residences, 528 commercial buildings, and 4,293 other structures. The tragic loss of life was compounded by the destruction not just of buildings but of what they contained: legal documents, financial records, medical files. Everything a person, family, business, or community needed to prove their rights and document their lives—gone.[7]

When I see news reports about a fire, flood, or earthquake, and I see a retired couple or a young family in tears, lamenting that they "lost everything," I feel my heart in my throat. Their "everything" was not their furniture, clothing, or pots and pans. Their "everything" was their family photographs, children's school reports, property documents, and medical records. Memories and evidence. Insurance companies will often replace a sofa or dining table with something else "just as good." Archives cannot be replaced with something else "just as good." When they are gone, they are gone, which is why it is so very important that we protect them from harm.

Retaining Evidence of Destruction

Is there anything worse than losing your family archives in a fire? Yes. Absolutely. A 450-square-mile area in northeastern France, known as the Zone Rouge or Red Zone, was the site of the Battle of Verdun in 1916, where more than 300,000 people died over the course of nine months. After the war, the area was littered with vast quantities of unexploded bombs, grenades, shells, and hazardous chemicals such as lead, mercury, and chlorine. The region was so badly damaged that the French government abandoned any thought of rehabilitation, opting instead to relocate people and cordon off the area. The government's Départment du Déminage (Department of Mine Clearances), established after World War II, regularly clears unexploded bombs and other ordnance from the fields and woods.[8]

How can a government protect people from such a toxic site? Erect a great big yellow "Keep Out" sign? Cordon off the area with a rope? (That's a lot of rope.) No. The way to protect people from such seriously dangerous places is to *keep records* of where those places are, what is wrong with them, and how the sites are being managed. People have the right to be protected from such life-threatening dangers. The government has an obligation to preserve an official account of the condition of the area, based on authentic and reliable sources of evidence. Ensuring that evidence is available for centuries into the future is critical to life and health.

There is a similar public obligation to preserve evidence about the location of nuclear waste and the condition of nuclear accident sites. Governments have to keep records of the level and nature of radioactivity at sites such as Three Mile Island, damaged in 1979, Chernobyl, in 1986, and Fukushima, in 2011. Members of the next generation—and the next and the next and the next—are going to depend for their lives on our ability to make and keep authentic, trust-worthy, and reliable documentary evidence of the state of these facilities right away, not a year or a decade from now. It is not enough to trust our memories. We need proof.

Unfortunately, in at least one case, this obligation was apparently not respected. In 2012, the Japanese government confirmed that it had not retained records of key meetings related to the 2011 Fukushima earthquake and tsunami. The government may have required that such records be created, and perhaps officials forgot; or the government may not have defined the kinds of evidence that should exist in response to a disaster, which meant no one knew what types of records to create. Either way, the records don't exist.

In the absence of authentic evidence, then Deputy Prime Minister Katsuya Okada had to instruct his ministers to produce after-the-fact summaries of meetings and discussions. How reliable will those summaries be? Isn't it bet-ter to capture that evidence at the time the meetings are held than to rely on personal memories later? Some would argue the lack of evidence is not just an oversight but an indication of negligence, with grave consequences.[9]

Using Evidence for History

The average person, of course, would not realize that government records relating to natural disasters or nuclear accidents do not exist, not until years or decades after the fact. Most people do not come face-to-face with original sources of evidence. They learn about events long after the fact, through a history book, radio broadcast, television documentary, or news report. The reading rooms of archival institutions are filled with countless numbers of historians and scholars who interpret recorded evidence in order to produce narrative accounts: depictions of historical events layered with interpretation and opinion. Historians are our intermediaries with the past, linking the general public and the original sources.

All history is *story*. It is not a definitive explanation of the past; it is only one person's perspective on that past. The type of historical narrative produced depends on the historian's interests and biases. One historian might use a collection of archives to write about justice and human rights. Another might use the same archives to consider concepts of identity and the evolution of communities. Still another might use the same evidence to present a political or economic argument.

If there was only one true, complete, definitive history, then Edward Gibbon's 18th-century colossus, *The History of the Decline and Fall of the Roman Empire*, would have remained our go-to source on the story of ancient Roman history. We wouldn't need Mary Beard. But Gibbon's wasn't the only history, and we do need Mary Beard. There are, what, 10,000 books on the Roman Empire? 20,000? How many articles? How many television documentaries? All of them depend on an analysis and interpretation of ever-changing sources of evidence. History is not proof. It's history.

The filmmaker Ken Burns has mined documentary evidence for nearly 40 years, from his first documentary film on the history of the Brooklyn Bridge in 1981 to his 2017 study of the Vietnam War. He has produced emotional and evocative historical accounts of the Statue of Liberty, the Civil War, baseball, jazz, Thomas Jefferson, Mark Twain, and Jackie Robinson. There is hardly a moment in any Ken Burns film that does not emerge from an analysis of some piece of evidence.

Historians like Gibbons or Beard or Burns may bring their own personal biases to their work, but they have an ethical obligation to respect the evidence found in documentary sources. To ensure they remain as trustworthy as possible, historians adhere to a set of objective professional standards. As stated in the American Historical Association's *Statement on Standards of Pro-*

fessional Conduct, "All historians believe in honoring the integrity of the historical record. They do not fabricate evidence."[10] John Adams, later America's second president, argued the same point in 1770. "Facts are stubborn things," he wrote, "and whatever may be our wishes, our inclinations, or the dictates of our passions, they cannot alter the state of facts and evidence."[11]

Still, we must always remember that the historian is presenting an interpretation, and that when we read that interpretation, we also bring our own biases to the task. Some say this is a postmodernist take on history. I think it is just a fact. We all have opinions—always have, always will. As Burns says, "History is a mysterious and malleable thing, constantly changing, not just as new information emerges, but as our own interests, emotions and inclinations change."[12]

It is important that we all read and think critically when presented with official narratives or historical accounts. But it is even more important that we continue to support the preservation of trustworthy evidence—not just the "old" stuff but the records and data we produce today, which will become the basis for historical accounts a hundred years from now.

Using Evidence for Journalism

Historical narratives are usually created long after the events in question. To shine a light on current events, we need journalists. And journalists depend on evidence. Unlike historians, though, journalists cannot wait for evidence to become "old" and settled. They are often chasing stories that change minute by minute. Journalists must move. Fast.

When Sean Spicer announced that Trump's inauguration was the largest ever, the journalists covering the story that week could not turn to ridership statistics summarized in the Metropolitan Area Transit Authority's official reports. Those reports didn't exist for another four months. Journalists use whatever "sources" they can access right away, from official communiqués, eyewitness accounts, and background papers to information from "leaks" and anonymous informants.

To help ensure they remain professional throughout this high-speed chase for facts, journalists establish strict protocols. Like historians, journalists are expected to act ethically. The Society of Professional Journalists' *Code of Ethics* outlines four core principles: seek truth and report it; minimize harm; act independently; and be accountable and transparent.[13] To uphold these principles, journalists keep detailed notes, verify their facts multiple times, and obtain legal advice before making confidential information public. Journalists may not carry the same devotion for the footnote as the historian (or the archivist—we *adore* footnotes), but good journalists authenticate their sources so they can produce not just any story but an evidence-based story. As argued by the Society of Professional Journalists' Ethics Committee, authenticity and credibility demand that journalists take an ethical approach to their work:

> Credibility is at the heart of journalism. The audience must believe the information it is receiving is accurate, the editorial judgments based on principles of fairness and balance. Sometimes, when faced with ethical choices for which there is no "right" answer, journalists can only follow a process that takes into account the interests of various "stakeholders," balances the public right to know against the privacy rights of individuals, the confidentiality needs of business and government, and reaches a considered judgment that the journalist believes is defensible. Or, one might say, a judgment they are willing to be held accountable for.[14]

Despite the existence of ethical frameworks, though, there is still such a thing as fake news. It has been around for centuries. As the historian Jacob Soll outlines, people were circulating false news reports well before Johannes Gutenberg unveiled his printing press in 1439. But Gutenberg's movable type made the process so much easier. Venetians circulated fake government reports in the 16th century. Catholics spread negative stories about Protestants in 18th-century France. A New York newspaper announced in 1835 that there was proof of life on the moon. George Washington's bogus proclamation in 1780 was fake news. During World War I, British writers such as Arthur Conan Doyle and H. G. Wells participated extensively in propaganda efforts, writing hundreds of pamphlets and books intended to promote the government's message while seeming to be neutral and objective. In World War II, the "Tokyo Rose" broadcasts spread Japanese propaganda to Allied troops in the South Pacific and North America. Fake news has always existed, and it always will.[15]

The grave danger today is not that reporters are lying. Some are, some aren't. That's not news. The real danger is that too many people cannot or will not distinguish between facts and lies. When people, especially people in power, claim that any statement contrary to their own perspective is fake news, their goal is not to tell the truth but to confuse and dissemble. At a political rally on July 24, 2018, Donald Trump told the audience, "Don't believe the crap you see from these people, the fake news. . . . What you're seeing and what you're reading is not what's happening." Trump's goal was to distract from the facts—the evidence-based facts—by appealing to emotions. This strategy is all too easy and far too successful these days.[16]

As more people choose instinct over evidence, they dismiss as a liar anyone who presents facts that contradict their feelings. When today's news is in your face every day on CNN or MSN or Fox or in 280-character bursts on your Twitter feed, journalists become an easy target. Again, the president of the United States has a lot to answer for here. On February 17, 2017, Donald Trump tweeted that the "fake news" media is "the enemy of the American People."[17] He has repeated the charge so often that the United Nations has criticized him in public for his attacks on the principle of a free press. The US Senate passed a resolution on August 16, 2018, stating that the media is not the enemy of the people. Still, on August 30, 2018, a California man was charged with threatening to kill reporters at *Boston Globe* after declaring, "You're the enemy of the people, and we're going to kill every f***ing one of you."[18]

It should be a long, long, long way from a Twitter message to murder. In 2019, it is not. As Lee McIntyre argues, "It's all fun and games to attack truth in the academy, but what happens when one's tactics leak out into the hands of science deniers and conspiracy theorists, or thin-skinned politicians who insist that their instincts are better than any evidence?"[19] Authentic and reliable sources of evidence will not save us from people who persist in lying, but if we do not protect the proof, then how will we even know that we are being lied to?

It was easy enough in the "olden days" to wait for benign neglect to sweep over a collection of paper archives in a dusty basement. If we just waited quietly for time to pass, archivists could step in later and gather the treasures, saving them for historians and posterity. What will be left for historians and posterity in the digital age? We need to act quickly to preserve our digital evidence so that it is safe, authentic, and accessible before it is lost, corrupted, or deleted. To act, people need to care.

I want people to care: to realize that their life stories are worth remembering, and that the evidence of their lives is worth preserving. History, journalism, family memories, and official narratives all depend on evidence. We are all richer when we can access not just after-the-fact stories but authentic sources of evidence, which can give such color, flavor, and meaning to the bare facts. I can only imagine that Ann Alsop would have preferred above all else that her father had not been killed in Burma in 1944. But what a gift she received instead, to hear John Hartley's voice and see him smiling and chirping . . . so very, very alive.

NOTES

1. For an account of the history of the film, see the book by Zapruder's granddaughter Alexandra Zapruder, *Twenty-Six Seconds: A Personal History of the Zapruder Film* (New York: Twelve, 2016). The museum is located in the building where Lee Harvey Oswald fired the bullet that killed President Kennedy.

2. The BBC RemArc website is available at http://remarc.bbcrewind.co.uk/index.html, *archived at* https://perma.cc/9T85-FAGU. The various clips are organized and displayed by theme or decade, although users can save the link to a particular clip for repeated viewing. A description of the RemArc initiative is available in a blog post from BBC Research and Development, "BBC RemArc—How Our Archives Can Help People with Dementia," February 27, 2017 (last updated February 2, 2018), https://www.bbc.co.uk/rd/blog/2017-02-bbc-rem-arc-dementia-memories-archive, *archived at* https://perma.cc/UZR7-STTT.

3. Ann Alsop's experience is discussed in Lindsay Pantry, "Re-discovered Film Footage Gives Emotional Insight into Life of Soldiers Fighting in the Far East," *Yorkshire Post*, June 27, 2016, https://www.yorkshirepost.co.uk/our-yorkshire/heritage/re-discovered -film-footage-gives-emotional-insight-into-life-of-soldiers-fighting-in-the-far-east -1-7981433, *archived at* https://perma.cc/FW8Y-SGQN. Ann Alsop is one of the family members included in UK Channel 4's 2016 documentary, *Messages Home: Lost Films of the British Army*, which discussed the discovery and preservation of the films and the plan to bring family members together to view them. See the project website at https://www.nwfa.mmu.ac.uk/blighty/Channel4doc.php, *archived at* https:// perma.cc/ZF92-F88P, and the Channel 4 website at https://www.channel4.com/ programmes/messages-home-lost-films-of-the-british-army/on-demand/62566-001, *archived at* https://perma.cc/RTD2-F2L9. See also Taukkyan War Cemetery, "Roll of Honour: Ha—United Kingdom," http://www.roll-of-honour.org.uk/cemeteries/ taukkyan_war_cemetery/h/html/ha.htm, *archived at* https://perma.cc/P25C-QE5H.

4. Paul Lewis, "Burning: The Evidence, How and Why Dickens Burned Tens of Thousands of Letters," *The Dickensian* 100, no. 464 (Winter 2004): 197–208.

5. See the finding aid and other descriptive information for the Hurston papers at the Department of Special & Area Studies Collections of the University of Florida George A. Smathers Libraries at http://www.uflib.ufl.edu/spec/aaexhibit/manuscripts .htm, *archived at* https://perma.cc/4VC9-SR6X, and http://www.library.ufl.edu/ spec/manuscript/hurston/hurston.htm, *archived at* https://perma.cc/GCL5-M8ZK.

6. The National Archives salvaged as much as it could, rescuing microfilm reels, computer databases, and any other evidence that might help reconstruct the original information. A description and analysis of the fire, "The 1973 Fire, National Personnel Records Center," is published on the NARA website at https://www.archives .gov/personnel-records-center/fire-1973, *archived at* https://perma.cc/7A3D-4B9F; see also Walter W. Stender and Evans Walker, "The National Personnel Records Center (NPRC) Fire: A Study in Disaster," *The American Archivist* 37, no. 4 (October 1974): 521–49, available as a download on the same web page.

7. A government report on the 2018 fire provides detailed information about the losses and the efforts to control the damage, along with recommendations to reduce the risk of wildfires in future; see State of California Watershed Emer-

gency Response Team, *Camp Fire: Watershed Emergency Response Team Final Report* (November 29, 2018), http://cdfdata.fire.ca.gov/pub/cdf/images/incident-file2277_4330.pdf, *archived at* https://perma.cc/ZC8S-Z6GP.

8. See Stuart Thornton, "Red Zone: France's Zone Rouge Is a Lingering Reminder of World War I," *National Geographic,* last updated May 1, 2015, https://www.national geographic.org/news/red-zone, *archived at* https://perma.cc/WEL6-BLBS. See also Shahan Russell, "The 'Red Zone' in France Is So Dangerous That 100 Years After WWI It Is Still a No-Go Area," *War History Online,* October 27, 2016, https://www.warhistory online.com/world-war-i/this-red-zone-in-france-is-so-dangerous-100-years-after-wwi -it-is-still-a-no-go-area.html, *archived at* https://perma.cc/BR3L-KZBF, and Danièle Voldman, "Le déminage de la France après 1945," *Les Chemins de la Mémoire,* no. 153 (September 2005), http://www.cheminsdememoire.gouv.fr/en/le-deminage-de-la -france-apres-1945, *archived at* https://perma.cc/3PM4-8JAC.

9. "Japan Did Not Keep Records of Nuclear Disaster Meetings," *BBC News,* January 27, 2012, https://www.bbc.com/news/world-asia-16754891, *archived at* https://perma .cc/4HLZ-EV88.

10. American Historical Association, *Statement on Standards of Professional Conduct* (updated July 2018), https://www.historians.org/jobs-and-professional-development/ statements-standards-and-guidelines-of-the-discipline/statement-on-standards-of -professional-conduct, *archived at* https://perma.cc/K8ZW-FZ22.

11. John Adams, "Adams' Argument for the Defense: 3–4 December 1770," in *The Trial of William Wemms, James Hartegan, William M'Cauley,* [and others] . . . *for the Murder of Crispus Attucks,* [and others] . . . *Superior Court of Judicature, Court of Assize, and General Goal Delivery . . . Taken in Short-Hand by John Hodgson* (Boston, 1770). For a digital copy, see the Library of Congress's Founders Online website at https:// founders.archives.gov/documents/Adams/05-03-02-0001-0004-0016, *archived at* https://perma.cc/59R6-8WT4.

12. Ken Burns, "Prepared Text of the 2016 Stanford Commencement Address by Ken Burns" (Stanford University, June 12, 2016), https://news.stanford.edu/2016/06 /12/prepared-text-2016-stanford-commencement-address-ken-burns, *archived at* https://perma.cc/2GWA-CTWM.

13. See the Society of Professional Journalists, *Code of Ethics* (revised September 6, 2014), https://www.spj.org/ethicscode.asp, *archived at* https://perma.cc/8DUX-ZLZP.

14. See the SPJ Ethics Committee's position paper on ethics and accountability at https://www.spj.org/ethics-papers-accountability.asp, *archived at* https://perma.cc/ M3Z3-Z534.

15. A great short analysis, by the historian Jacob Soll, is "The Long and Brutal History of Fake News," *Politico Magazine,* December 18, 2016, https://www.politico.com/magazine/ story/2016/12/fake-news-history-long-violent-214535, *archived at* https://perma.cc/ GWP9-AKFX. One of the classic analyses of World War I and post-war propaganda is Peter Buitenhuis, *The Great War of Words: British, American, and Canadian Propaganda and Fiction, 1914–1933* (Vancouver: University of British Columbia Press, 1987). A useful overview of Japanese propaganda in World War II comes from Barak Kushner, *The Thought War: Japanese Imperial Propaganda* (Honolulu: The University of Hawaii Press, 2007).

16. Reported in Chris Cillizza, "Donald Trump Just Said Something Truly Terrifying," *CNN Politics*, July 25, 2018, https://www.cnn.com/2018/07/25/politics/donald-trump-vfw-unreality/index.html, *archived at* https://perma.cc/MT7U-UB6Q.

17. See Donald Trump's tweet at https://twitter.com/realdonaldtrump/status/832708293516632065?lang=en, *archived at* https://perma.cc/73UZ-YC5W.

18. There are dozens of media reports on this story, one of which is by National Public Radio's Amy Held; see "'Enemy of the People': Man Echoing Trump's Words Charged with Threatening Newspaper," *NPR Media*, August 30, 2018, https://www.npr.org/2018/08/30/643377599/enemy-of-the-people-man-echoing-trump-s-words-charged-with-threatening-newspaper, *archived at* https://perma.cc/TMF9-BMTX.

19. Lee McIntyre, *Post-Truth* (Cambridge, MA: MIT Press, 2018), 145.

8

"Opinions embedded in math"

Evidence, Manipulation, and Abuse

A lie, turned topsy-turvy, can be prinked and tinselled out, decked
in plumage new and fine, till none knows its lean old carcass.

Henrik Ibsen, 1876

ACCORDING TO JOURNALIST DEBBIE NATHAN OF *THE INTERCEPT*, US
Customs and Border Protection—the agency responsible for securing American borders—claimed that its agents had experienced a 73 percent increase in assaults in 2017. That number, she argued, had been inflated significantly. The data showed that in February 2017, for instance, seven agents reported being assaulted by six subjects, and that three different types of weapons were used: rocks, bottles, and tree branches. Even though the agency might reasonably have calculated this incident as seven assaults, one against each agent, Customs and Border Protection instead calculated it as 126 assaults: 7 agents × 6 perpetrators × 3 projectiles. Is this a miscalculation of data or a manipulation of evidence?[1]

Just as evidence can be used, it can be misused, particularly when facts and statements are aggregated into summaries and statistics. But at the heart of any statistical analysis is (or ought to be) a piece of evidence: verifiable proof of an act, event, transaction, or communication. Only when acts become facts and facts are documented as evidence can we analyze those acts and facts with authority. As Sir Joseph Stamp, a British economist and Director of the Bank of England, wrote in 1922, "Every time that we die or get married or have babies we get into some statistical mill or other, and our height and our health and our habits, and almost our hopes, are raw material for politicians, economists and taproom orators."[2]

When we read statistical reports, we want to believe that the sources of proof are verifiable, that the aggregate information has been compiled accurately, and that the conclusions are based on objective and impartial analysis. But it doesn't always work that way. It is not wise to assume that the evidence behind statistics is always authentic and complete or that the resulting analyses are inevitably impartial and objective. It is also dangerous to believe that evidence is safe from manipulation or theft. Evidence can be stolen and leaked, revealing our private selves to the world without our permission. Computers can be programmed to interpret and misinterpret the facts without our knowledge or consent. And it only takes one simple but lethal computer virus to lock down vital information systems, holding our sources of evidence hostage. We need to ensure evidence is used as a tool, not a weapon.

Playing with Numbers

In 1998, the British gastroenterologist Andrew Wakefield authored a paper for the prominent medical journal *The Lancet* in which he argued that the measles, mumps, rubella (MMR) vaccine was directly linked to incidences of colitis and autism in the children he studied. Wakefield's controversial argument spread like a disease. As more and more parents stopped vaccinating their children, the United Kingdom saw a marked increase in the number of confirmed cases of measles: from 56 in 1998 to 971 in 2007.[3]

Subsequent epidemiological studies showed no link between the MMR vaccine and autism. Investigative journalist Brian Deer then uncovered proof that Wakefield had both manipulated his original sources of evidence and falsified his results. According to Deer, Wakefield studied only 12 children. Even then, he did not document their symptoms accurately or completely. Some children did not have autism at all, and others had preexisting conditions that Wakefield did not factor into his analysis. As well, negative test results were changed to imply there was disease present when none had been found. In 2004, Wakefield's paper was partially retracted. In 2010, it was fully retracted, and Wakefield was barred from practicing medicine in the United Kingdom. But too much time passed before Wakefield's lies caught up with him. Children died of preventable diseases before he was stopped. And children continue to suffer and die. In April 2019, the Centers for Disease Control and Prevention reported that the United States was facing the second-greatest number of measles cases since the disease had (so everyone believed) been eliminated in 2000: 555 individual cases in 20 states from January 1 to April 11, 2019. As parents reject vaccines as unnatural and link them to a debunked theory about autism, their children are increasingly vulnerable to a deadly disease. We shouldn't have to depend on physical evidence, in the form of sick and dying children, to know vaccines work, when we already have trustworthy scientific and documentary proof of the fact.[4]

Statistics should be based on verifiable facts and authentic evidence. Saying that 90 percent of people polled would vote for Candidate Jacobs is deceitful if the poll was conducted in the middle of a "Vote for Jacobs" pep rally in the local gym. Saying that one out of every two housewives prefers Tide is dubious if the sample size is two. Claiming that murder rates in Smithville doubled in a year is provocative if there was only one murder in the town in 2017 and never a murder before then.

Ethical statisticians know this. They draw on authentic and verifiable sources of evidence, use transparent and reproducible methodologies, and replace assumptions with analyses. The American Statistical Association's *Ethical Guidelines for Statistical Practice* requires that professional statisticians always remain accountable for their work; maintain professional integrity when gathering and assessing data; and provide the highest respect for science and the public as well as for funders, clients, and colleagues. As the ASA argues,

> The discipline of statistics links the capacity to observe with the ability to gather evidence and make decisions, providing a foundation for building a more informed society. Because society depends on informed judgments supported by statistical methods, all practitioners of statistics—regardless of training and occupation or job title—have an obligation to work in a professional, competent, respectful, and ethical manner.[5]

Frauds like Wakefield probably skipped the section on ensuring the integrity of source data and analyzing the findings accurately. Lies, damn lies, and statistics indeed.[6]

Leaking or Liberating?

The trustworthiness of evidence is also endangered when sources are taken out of their original context. Whether that removal is necessary might be a matter of perspective. In 2010, Chelsea (then Bradley) Manning released hundreds of thousands of documents related to US Army activities in Iraq and Afghanistan, making the evidence available to WikiLeaks to publish. In 2013, Edward Snowden copied and leaked classified documents from the National Security Agency. The Paradise Papers leak in 2017 released more than 13 million digital records related to offshore financial investments by major corporations, including Facebook, Twitter, Apple, and Disney.[7] Were they leakers, whistleblowers, or justice warriors?

We may applaud when people release evidence that shows that the "bad guys" really were bad and that the "good guys" really were good. But who is to say that we, or the liberators/thieves, are right? We may see a whole bunch of angels on our side, but does the end—the disclosure of otherwise secret evidence—justify the means—breaking the law and violating people's rights and privacy? It is not a simple yes or no question.

As I discussed earlier, WikiLeaks claimed in 2015 that it had published more than 10 million documents. Since then it has published millions more, from Russian companies, American embassies, the Catholic Church, and dozens of other sources.[8] Some of the evidence released proves that governments and corporations have not been operating in the best interests of the public. But the leaks have also made available some highly sensitive personal information, including the identities of otherwise anonymous sources of information, such as undercover agents. WikiLeaks has been praised by some for forcing those in power to reveal secrets and condemned by others for breaching privacy and endangering lives. The arrest of Julian Assange in April 2019 on charges of conspiracy opens the lid on this particular can of worms. His trial (assuming the case goes to trial) will initiate a discussion of whether WikiLeaks is liberator or thief. Is WikiLeaks a publisher, disseminating government information obtained from other sources—a legal if sometimes morally challenging activity? Or is WikiLeaks complicit in the illegal act of hacking computers and stealing confidential government documents? Whether Assange will be found culpable will, fittingly yet ironically, be decided in large part on an analysis of evidence.[9]

The Panama Papers leak, which released over 11 million documents from the Panamanian law firm Mossack Fonseca, provided proof of a web of offshore accounts and tax evasion. The anonymous "John Doe" who published the Panama Papers in 2015 explained his motivation to make available what he believed to be incriminating evidence, arguing that "historians can easily recount how issues involving taxation and imbalances of power have led to revolutions in ages past. Then, military might was necessary to subjugate peoples, whereas now, curtailing information access is just as effective or more so, since the act is often invisible."[10]

John Doe is right. Governments and organizations with power *can* withhold evidence from the public simply by ignoring existing evidence laws or by refusing to implement legislation that requires the creation and preservation of authentic records. They can also manipulate technology, hide records, and alter evidence. They do it all the time. They always have, which is why stealing/liberating evidence in order to expose government secrets is nothing new.

The South African History Archive in Johannesburg began life in the 1980s when a group of activists, seeking to expose the truth of apartheid, began filing access to information requests with the South African government and then making the documents they received available to the public. The Washington-based National Security Archive was founded by journalists and scholars to fight government secrecy by publishing records received through access requests. In 1971, military analyst Daniel Ellsberg photocopied thousands of pages of government records and leaked them to the press; the Pentagon Papers revealed that the US government was deliberately deceiving the public about America's role in the Vietnam War. In 1934, German government press officer Herbert von Bose was assassinated after he was caught leaking secret information about the Nazi Party to English journalists. He was trying to show the world how severely the Nazis were disrespecting not only the law but the rule of law. The Irish "saved civilization" in the 10th and 11th centuries, some say, when hooded monks slipped off with fragile and sensitive manuscripts and copied them, rescuing small pieces of documentary evidence from the void of the Dark Ages. Rescue or theft? Revelation or exposé? Glass half full or glass half empty?[11]

The problem with leaks is that in an ideal world, they wouldn't need to happen at all. Governments would establish reasonable, sensible laws, and then they would abide by them. People in power would make and keep good records—trustworthy evidence—of their actions and decisions, and they would make that evidence available to the public with only a minimum of control. If evidence were well made, well kept, and consistently accessible, with the balance in favor of access over privacy, why would anyone need to steal it?

When that ideal does not exist, what is the next best thing? If someone is going to rescue/steal evidence, three conditions should apply. First, the whistleblower/thief (glass half full/glass half empty) should act only with the most honorable of intentions. Transparency. Truth. Righteousness. But who can say that my intentions are honorable? I may believe my motivations are beyond pure. You may think I am evil incarnate. In this regard, one has to question the motivation behind the WikiLeaks decision to release a searchable archive of some 30,000 of Hillary Clinton's emails in March 2016, in the thick of the US presidential election. Transparency? Truth? Honor? According to the evidence presented in the 2019 Mueller report, Assange called Clinton a bright, well-connected, sadistic sociopath, arguing that "we believe it would be much better for GOP to win. . . . With Hillary in charge, GOP will be pushing for her worst qualities . . . dems+media+neoliberals will be mute."[12] Doesn't seem terribly honorable to me.

The second condition is that the thief/leaker should do everything possible to ensure the trustworthiness of the evidence in question. Of course, the very act of removing evidence changes it completely. Police officers and lawyers (and archivists) strive to maintain an unbroken chain of custody precisely in order to protect the integrity of the evidence. Otherwise, how can we know that evidence removed from its original context is authentic? How do we know that 30,000 emails are *all* the emails, or the *right* emails, or the *only* emails? Or that they have been left intact—complete and unedited—with sufficient contextual information to ensure they can stand as proof?

The third condition is that the person leaking the evidence should make every effort to respect an individual's personal privacy. Society may benefit if a whistleblower exposes government corruption, but where is the public good in publishing a public servant's home address, or her spouse's cell phone number, or the name of her child's school?

Stealing and leaking evidence should be an extreme measure, used only in extreme cases. One such case, I would argue, involves the war in Syria, under way since 2011. An activist group called the Commission for International Justice and Accountability (CIJA) is smuggling hundreds of thousands of records of the Ba'ath Party Government out of the country to preserve authentic evidence that might someday be used to demonstrate that President Bashar al-Assad's government has committed war crimes. To remove evidence from the country, operatives have taped records to their bodies, hidden data-filled flash drives in their socks, and wrapped paper documents in plastic wrap to hide them away. When unable to remove evidence immediately, agents have buried records in boxes in undisclosed locations around the country. As of 2016, it was estimated that a half a million pages of documents have been secreted in holes and caves in the Syrian desert, waiting to be retrieved when the war ends.

One of the central tenets of the smuggling operation is that everyone involved must do all they can to document the chain of custody fully, to make it as difficult as possible for a defense lawyer to claim that files have been tampered with or contents destroyed. As Stephen Rapp, the former US Ambassador-at-Large for War Crimes Issues, has argued, the emphasis on chain of custody helps ensure that the stolen CIJA records will provide "much better evidence than we've had anywhere since Nuremberg."[13]

Of course, the ideal solution would be to end the war. But when that happens, we cannot just dust ourselves off and hope it doesn't happen again. The victims of war deserve justice. And justice demands evidence. If stealing and leaking are necessary in order to secure the evidence needed to judge the per-petrators fairly and fully, so that those responsible can be punished, perhaps that is better than doing nothing at all. But if you're going to steal, for heaven's sake, do it right.

Endangering Privacy

Whistleblowers can violate a person's privacy by leaking evidence indiscrimi-nately. But our privacy is imperiled every time we use computer technologies to share information with each other. Whenever we post a message on Facebook, add a photograph to Instagram, or email our travel itinerary to the house sit-ter, we risk exposing ourselves to the world. Yet here we are, embracing every new piece of computer technology like a long-lost lover, only to be horrified whenever we hear of computer failures or data breaches, which happen with alarming frequency.

In April 2019, journalists reported that thousands of Amazon employees have been actively listening to conversations recorded on the company's Alexa devices (voice-controlled "smart" speakers that can be used to play music or answer questions). Apparently, employees listen to voice recordings captured in offices and private homes, transcribe the recordings, annotate them, then feed the words back into the Alexa software in order to improve how the device understands and responds to human speech. They aren't *really* listening to us, are they? They are just interested in the words. Not the content. Right? One could argue this is an innocent attempt to improve technology. Others could say it is a slick slope downward, to a world where privacy is perpetually at risk. Will we have any personal space anymore, when our "smart" speakers, refriger-ators, and garage door openers can spy on us?[14]

In Norway, a computer start-up called No Isolation has developed a robot that acts as an avatar, replacing an ill child in the classroom. The robot sits in the classroom while the little boy or girl stays at home and recovers. The child can hear and see the teacher and classmates through the "eyes" of the robot and can communicate through the microphone and speakers. The goal, honorable in principle, is to foster social inclusion. But how much can we trust that the technology will operate as intended? The teacher will need to ensure that any evidence generated by the technology remains secure. The students will need to be reminded that they should be as kind to the avatar as they would be if the child were with them in person. Still, what is to prevent someone from hacking into the avatar, pretending to be another child, or a teacher or family member, and using the tool to abuse the child?[15]

The answer is not to stop using technology. The answer is to remember that the "data" we generate every day might well be evidence, and then to protect that evidence so that it can be used to help us, not harm us. The challenge is to be more circumspect about how, when, and why we use information technologies, and less tolerant when governments, corporations, and hostile forces misuse technology, mismanage evidence, and abuse trust.

Neglecting Evidence

In 2010, *CBS News* reported that 6,000 used photocopiers were sitting in a New Jersey warehouse waiting to be sold. On each of those machines was a hard drive, and on each of those hard drives was a digital version of every document that had been copied, scanned, or emailed by the machine. One of the photocopiers still had a document on the glass from the police department's sex crimes division in Buffalo, New York. The hard drive for that machine also contained other highly sensitive police records.[16] We wouldn't take a refrigerator out of our kitchen without first disposing of the food inside, would we? Why would we dispose of a piece of equipment solely intended to manage evidence without first checking that the evidence had been removed appropriately?

A similar case of neglect (abuse?) in Australia involved a 2013 digitization project by the BT Financial Group, an arm of the Australian bank Westpac. During the project, officials realized that some 10,000 of its customer files were missing. Some 8,000 were in regional branches, but the remaining 2,000 had to be re-created from other files. (BT Financial Group disputed the numbers, saying only 215 files were lost.) A subsequent Royal Commission into the banking industry noted that Westpac had demonstrated "exceedingly poor management of client file records." It was worse than "poor," actually. One of the investigators called the recordkeeping failure "the worst we have seen in recent times."[17]

Privacy can be violated even when the technology is not shiny and new, as happened in Fort Worth, Texas, in 2013. The Texas Health Harris Methodist Hospital advised 277,000 patients of a potential privacy breach after microfiche copies of old medical records were found in a public dumpster. The records were supposed to have been destroyed by a third-party contractor, but they had been tossed in the garbage instead.[18] One would hope that the contractor could be sued for neglect or mismanagement. But if the service agreement does not explicitly state that documentary evidence must be destroyed securely, what's to stop any contractor from pitching records or microfilms or computer disks in the trash? If organizations are not required to ensure their sources of evidence are protected, how can we the public ensure our own privacy is secure? We need to demand better from those who hold evidence in our name, whether they are governments, corporations, or digital service providers.

Trusting Algorithms

The risks to privacy and to the integrity of evidence will only increase as technology grows more sophisticated. When Cambridge Analytica scraped "data" from Facebook users in the United Kingdom, it gained access to evidence: names and addresses, birthdays, and hometowns. The evidence could be used to find out where someone worked, where his or her children went to school, or when the family left on holiday. What is to stop people from using our evidence for disinformation campaigns, unwanted fundraising, covert surveillance, political interference, or racial profiling?

In 2016, the Government Accountability Office, or GAO, investigated the use of facial recognition technology by the US Federal Bureau of Investigation. The FBI had collected images of over 30 million people; about 70 percent of the images were mugshots of criminals. The FBI then used algorithms to match the facial characteristics of someone against a "candidate," such as a potential or an actual criminal. The processes that determined whose faces were captured and analyzed were inconsistent, to put it mildly. In its report, which some referred to as "scathing," the GAO criticized the FBI for the lack of internal controls and the consequent risks to personal privacy. The GAO called on the FBI and other agencies to improve significantly their privacy protections and audit processes.[19]

Big data is the holy grail for governments, market researchers, major corporations, and political campaigners. To make use of "big data" sets that result from the aggregation of massive quantities of digital information, researchers need access to reams of evidence, which they then analyze using a variety of algorithms. They can end up with answers to questions about us that we did not even know they were asking. In his book *Everybody Lies*, Seth Stephens-Davidowitz gives an account of what happens when banks use big data to assess loan applications. In the mythical "good old days" (imagine George Bailey in *It's a Wonderful Life*), a local bank manager might lend money to an applicant on the strength of her promise to repay. "She's a good bet," George would have said. But as Stephens-Davidowitz explains, if you take a huge accumulation of loan applications (which are evidence, not just information) and then enter the data from those applications into a database, you can apply algorithms to come up with some startling results. According to the math, the applications from people more likely to pay back their loans included words like "debt-free," "graduate," or "minimum payment." The applications from people more likely to default on their loans included words such as "God," "promise," and "thank you."[20]

Did the people who filled out the application forms think their requests would be judged by an algorithm? If they knew their words would be parsed by a computer, perhaps they would have structured their applications differently, adding words or phrases that might improve their chances of success. If they do that, are they still telling the truth? Or are they spinning their story to get the best results? Can they even tell the difference anymore? Using algorithms to analyze and manipulate evidence may be the wave of the future. But it's a powerful wave, and it threatens to wreak destruction when it hits the shore. As data scientist Cathy O'Neil says, "Algorithms are opinions embedded in math."[21] If we are going to maintain some measure of integrity and trustworthiness across society, we need to remember that our data can serve as evidence. We need to decide for ourselves whether and how we will use technology to create, interpret, and use that evidence.

Hijacking Evidence

On May 12, 2017, a computer worm called WannaCry hit more than 230,000 computers in over 150 countries, encrypting computer files. Suddenly, no one whose computer was infected could access their digital data or records. The hackers responsible for WannaCry demanded payments in bitcoin cryptocurrency before they would release the locked-down files. It took nearly a month for the attack to diminish and for businesses to start restoring normal operations. One of the agencies badly affected by the attack was the United Kingdom's National Health Service, which was forced to cancel over 9,000 medical appointments and procedures because it could not access patient records.[22]

A much more destructive cyberattack happened in 2017, with the release of a piece of ransomware called NotPetya (so named because it was a variant of an already known malware called Petya, first launched in 2016). NotPetya was infinitely more insidious than WannaCry. Once a computer was attacked by NotPetya, the payment of a ransom would make no difference; the data simply could not be recovered.

The NotPetya attack affected banks, government offices, and transit systems, and businesses in France, Italy, and the United Kingdom, but the highest incidence of infection took place in Russia and Ukraine. Technology experts believe the attack was politically motivated, to harm Ukraine, which has been at war with Russia since 2014. Among the other agencies hit were the American pharmaceutical corporation Merck & Co., the German logistics firm DHL, and Maersk, the largest shipping company in the world, which claimed a loss of $870 million in income. It took Maersk over two weeks to reestablish basic computer connections, and even then, the company could not resurrect its digital records. It lost all access to evidence of the location, contents, destinations, and status of shipping containers all around the world. More frightening, NotPetya also shut down the radiation monitoring system at Ukraine's Chernobyl nuclear power plant, which is still radioactive more than 30 years after the catastrophic nuclear accident in April 1986.[23]

What makes the story even more alarming (as if things could get worse) is that NotPetya was built from a piece of computer code that had been stolen from the National Security Agency, America's spy agency. Apparently, the NSA collects rogue codes, viruses, and worms to analyze them and develop counterattacks. That makes sense, I guess. How can you combat a hostile force if you do not understand it? But the NSA's systems were hacked in 2017, and the evidence was stolen.

It is hard to know whether and how an attack such as NotPetya could have been prevented. But if nuclear facilities can be shut down in an instant and the operations of a multi-billion-dollar company brought to a standstill simply because someone turned on an office computer one Tuesday morning, then it is not good enough for people to suggest, as I have heard far too often, "Why don't you just turn off the Internet, or back up everything on USB sticks, or print everything out?" If whole societies are going to place the lives and livelihood of their citizens in the hands of machines, we need a better backup plan than pulling the plug.

Back when people put photographs in bound albums and wrote letters by hand, it was easier to make sure the evidence was safe, authentic, and unchanged. Now we use the Internet and social media to share everything from job applications to pictures of our breakfast. Governments store their official records in the cloud. Families and community groups use Facebook to exchange stories and pictures. It is so easy. It seems so safe. But have we placed too much trust in the tools? How can we combat manipulation and abuse and ensure our sources of evidence are protected from attack?

We need to find some way to balance convenience with security, which means we need to shed some of our assumptions about the nature of evidence.

Imagine if we were as relaxed with our automobiles as we are with our computers. We may want to hop into our car and take off at a moment's notice. But that doesn't mean we park the car in the driveway with the keys in the ignition and the engine running. If we did, would we have any reason to complain when a thief drove off in our car? In broad daylight?

NOTES

1. See Debbie Nathan, "How the Border Patrol Faked Statistics Showing a 73 Percent Rise in Assaults against Agents," *The Intercept*, April 23, 2018, https://theintercept .com/2018/04/23/border-patrol-agents-assaulted-cbp-fbi, *archived at* https:// perma.cc/U3RV-8DCF.

2. Sir Joseph Stamp, *Some Economic Factors in Modern Life* (London: P. S. King & Son, 1922), 253.

3. Wakefield's original paper, with S. H. Murch, A. Anthony, et al., is "Ileal-Lymphoid -Nodular Hyperplasia, Non-specific Colitis, and Pervasive Developmental Disorder in Children," *The Lancet* 351, no. 9103 (1998): 637–41. See also Peter McIntyre and Julie Leask, "Improving Uptake of MMR Vaccine," *British Medical Journal* 336 (2008): 729–30, https://www.bmj.com/content/336/7647/729, *archived at* https:// perma.cc/P6WQ-AAC6.

4. See Brian Deer, "How the Case against the MMR Vaccine Was Fixed," *British Medical Journal* 342 (2011): c5347, https://doi.org/10.1136/bmj.c5347, *archived at* https:// perma.cc/JY6T-PLYE. See also PBS, "The Vaccine War," *Frontline*, April 27, 2010, https://www.pbs.org/wgbh/frontline/film/vaccines, *archived at* https://perma.cc/ 3PTQ-T7YX. The Centers for Disease Control and Prevention provides up-to-date statistics and associated evidence on its website at https://www.cdc.gov/measles/ cases-outbreaks.html, *archived at* https://perma.cc/H6DK-VXNS.

5. See Committee on Professional Ethics, American Statistical Association, *Ethical Guidelines for Statistical Practice* (approved by the ASA Board of Directors, April 14, 2018), https://www.amstat.org/asa/files/pdfs/EthicalGuidelines.pdf, *archived at* https://perma.cc/X4NL-B8YX.

6. I am grateful to John McDonald for sharing his research on the relationship between statistics and evidence, published in *A Matter of Trust: Records as the Foundation for Building Integrity and Accountability into Data and Statistics to Support the UN Sustainable Development Goals—Concepts, Issues and Potential Strategies* (London: Institute of Commonwealth Studies, 2018), https://sas-space.sas.ac.uk/ 9179, *archived at* https://perma.cc/J5VP-N3RU.

7. The International Consortium of Investigative Journalists' account of the Paradise Papers can be seen on the ICIJ website at https://www.icij.org/investigations/ paradise-papers, *archived at* https://perma.cc/88Y7-74CU. Intriguingly, the website includes not only "Support us" and "Follow us" links but also a link for "Leak to us." They certainly make it as easy as possible.

8. "We Are Drowning in Material," interview of Julian Assange by Germany's Michael Sontheimer, *Spiegel Online*, July 20, 2015, http://www.spiegel.de/international/

world/spiegel-interview-with-wikileaks-head-julian-assange-a-1044399.html, *archived at* https://perma.cc/HE9U-3WZU. A review of the WikiLeaks home page shows the wide range of documents gathered from diverse sources; see https://wikileaks.org, *archived at* https://perma.cc/RDE9-HTWL.

9. See James Ball, "WikiLeaks Publishes Full Cache of Unredacted Cables," *The Guardian*, September 2, 2011, https://www.theguardian.com/media/2011/sep/02/wikileaks-publishes-cache-unredacted-cables, *archived at* https://perma.cc/M62B-JHFJ. See also William Booth, Ellen Nakashima, James McAuley, and Matt Zapotosky, "WikiLeaks' Assange Arrested in London, Accused by U.S. of Conspiring in 2010 Computer Hacking Attempt," *The Washington Post*, April 11, 2019, https://www.washingtonpost.com/world/europe/wikileakss-julian-assange-evicted-from-ecuador-embassy-in-london/2019/04/11/1bd87b58-8f5f-11e8-ae5901880eac5f1d_story.html?utm_term=.9a6c0bed1914, *archived at* https://perma.cc/9R4B-WNYK. Manning, an alleged WikiLeaks co-conspirator, was sentenced to 35 years in prison, a sentence later commuted by President Barack Obama; see Charlie Savage, "Chelsea Manning to Be Released Early as Obama Commutes Sentence," *The New York Times*, January 17, 2017, https://www.nytimes.com/2017/01/17/us/politics/obama-commutes-bulk-of-chelsea-mannings-sentence.html, *archived at* https://perma.cc/PU8C-5GU5.

10. See "Statement from Panama Papers Source," *The New York Times*, May 6, 2016, https://www.nytimes.com/interactive/2016/05/06/world/panama-papers-source-statement.html, *archived at* https://perma.cc/9M56-ZAFJ and https://perma.cc/N59B-RQHU.

11. For more information on the South African History Archive, see SAHA's website at www.saha.org.za, *archived at* https://perma.cc/ZBW9-VTPL, and to learn more about the National Security Archive, see its website at https://nsarchive.gwu.edu, *archived at* https://perma.cc/6TCU-XQC9. The Pentagon Papers story has been told many times; for Ellsberg's own perspective, see Daniel Ellsberg, *Secrets: A Memoir of Vietnam and the Pentagon Papers* (New York: Viking, 2002). For a recent discussion of the events surrounding Nazi activities in the interwar years, see Barry A. Jackish, ed., *The Pan-German League and Radical Nationalist Politics in Interwar Germany, 1918–39* (London: Routledge, 2012). One of the most popular books on the history of medieval Irish scholarship is by Thomas Cahill, *How the Irish Saved Civilization: The Untold Story of Ireland's Heroic Role from the Fall of Rome to the Rise of Medieval Europe* (New York: Anchor Books, 1996).

12. Special Counsel Robert S. Mueller III, *Report on the Investigation into Russian Interference in the 2016 Presidential Election* (Washington, DC: US Department of Justice, March 2019), vol. I, pp. 44–45, https://www.justice.gov/sco, *archived at* https://perma.cc/LQY3-MPVG, as published by *The New York Times* at https://www.nytimes.com/interactive/2019/04/18/us/politics/mueller-report-document.html, *archived at* https://perma.cc/GHN7-2AYF.

13. The official website for the CIJA is at https://cja.org, *archived at* https://perma.cc/Z3XG-SNFH. An account of the CIJA's efforts to document Syrian war crimes is detailed by award-winning journalist Ben Taub in "The Assad Files: Capturing the Top-Secret Documents That Tie the Syrian Regime to Mass Torture and Killings,"

The New Yorker, April 18, 2016, https://www.newyorker.com/magazine/2016/ 04/18/bashar-al-assads-war-crimes-exposed, *archived at* https://perma.cc/ EEU9-5AKF.

14. Matt Day, Giles Turner, and Natalia Drozdiak, "Amazon Workers Are Listening to What You Tell Alexa," *Bloomberg*, April 10, 2019, https://www.bloomberg.com/news/articles/2019-04-10/is-anyone-listening-to-you-on-alexa-a-global-team-reviews-audio, *archived at* https://perma.cc/YH5P-KHA8.

15. See Ellen Tsang's report for the BBC, "The Little Robot Helping Ill Kids Stay Connected," in *The Cultural Frontline: How Can We Design a Better World*, prod. BBC World Service, https://www.bbc.co.uk/programmes/p06lllj8, *archived at* https://perma.cc/9RAL-7U25.

16. See Armien Keteyian, "Digital Photocopiers Loaded with Secrets," *CBS Evening News*, April 19, 2010, https://www.cbsnews.com/news/digital-photocopiers-loaded-with-secrets, *archived at* https://perma.cc/SJ2F-KBTB. See also Emily Rand, "CBS News Investigation into Photocopiers Raises Questions in Buffalo," *CBS Evening News*, April 20, 2010, https:// www.cbsnews.com/news/cbs-news-investigation-into-photocopiers-raises-questions-in -buffalo, *archived at* https://perma.cc/33N7-EFYE.

17. Christopher Knaus, "Westpac Lost Files of Hundreds of Clients, Whistleblowers Say," *The Guardian* (Australia), June 3, 2018, https://www.theguardian.com/australia-news/2018/ jun/03/westpac-lost-files-of-hundreds-of-clients-whistleblowers-say, *archived at* https:// perma.cc/B9BE-YJPN. See also the transcript of proceedings of the Royal Commission, The Honourable K. Hayne AC QC, Commissioner, *In the Matter of a Royal Commission into Misconduct in the Banking, Superannuation and Financial Services Industry* (Melbourne, 9:30 a.m., Thursday, April 19, 2018), https://financialservices.royalcommission.gov.au/public -hearings/Documents/transcripts-2018/transcript-19-april-2018.pdf, *archived at* https:// perma.cc/4YJ9-GWSU.

18. Marianne Kolbasuk McGee, "Texas Breach Affects 277,000: Microfiche Records Slated for Destruction Found in Dumpster," *Healthcare Info Security*, July 12, 2013, https://www .healthcareinfosecurity.com/texas-breach-affects-277000-a-5908, *archived at* https:// perma.cc/22GF-NT8Q.

19. See GAO, *Face Recognition Technology: FBI Should Better Ensure Privacy and Accuracy* (Report to the Ranking Member, Subcommittee on Privacy, Technology and the Law, Committee on the Judiciary, U.S. Senate, GAO-16-267, May 2016), http://www.gao.gov/assets/ 680/677098.pdf, *archived at* https://perma.cc/6CTJ-F5R9. See also Jennifer Lynch, *Face Off: Law Enforcement Use of Face Recognition Technology* (San Francisco: Electronic Frontier Foundation, February 12, 2018), https://www.eff.org/files/2018/02/15/face-off-report -1b.pdf, *archived at* https://perma.cc/MB9Q-7QLM.

20. See Seth Stephens-Davidowitz, *Everybody Lies: Big Data, New Data, and What the Internet Can Tell Us about Who We Really Are* (New York: HarperCollins, 2017), esp. 258–61. Another analysis of the challenge of using algorithms is Safiya Umoja Nobile, *Algorithms of Oppression: How Search Engines Reinforce Racism* (New York: New York University Press, 2018).

21. Cathy O'Neil, interviewed in the BBC World Service podcast "How Powerful Is Facebook's Algorithm?," *The Inquiry*, April 19, 2017, https://www.bbc.co.uk/programmes/p04zvqtx, *archived at* https://perma.cc/P5T9-Q97S.

22. A breakdown of the WannaCry attack and an analysis of the security issues were published by the BBC in October 2017. See "NHS 'Could Have Prevented' WannaCry Ransomware Attack," *BBC News*, October 27, 2017, https://www.bbc.com/news/technology-41753022, *archived at* https://perma.cc/QN3Z-CGFK; see as well the analysis by Rory Cellan-Jones that follows on the same web page. See also David Navin, "What the NHS Could Learn from 2017's WannaCry Attack," *IFSEC Global*, July 30, 2018, https://www.ifsecglobal.com/nhs-learn-2017s-wannacry, *archived at* https://perma.cc/6MSF-LKYS.

23. An excellent if frightening analysis of the NotPetya malware attack is Andy Greenberg's "The Code That Crashed the World," *Wired* (September 2018): 53–63.

9

"Electronic records, paper minds"
Evidence and Assumptions

> *Assumptions are dangerous things to make, and like all dangerous things to make—bombs, for instance, or strawberry shortcake—if you make even the tiniest mistake you can find yourself in terrible trouble.*
> Lemony Snicket, n.d.

THE PRESIDENT OF THE UNITED STATES IS BOUND BY SECTION 3 OF the Constitution to "take care that the Laws be faithfully executed." The president is also bound by the Presidential Records Act to preserve official records of his time in office. Only the National Archivist can authorize the destruction of presidential records.[1] By all accounts, President Trump is ignoring these obligations. According to reports by the news magazine *Politico*, the management of White House memos, emails, speeches, telephone logs, and Twitter messages is "haphazard," and President Trump actively avoids using official email or other communications systems. As he noted before he took office, "If you have something really important, write it out and have it delivered by courier, the old-fashioned way. . . . No computer is safe." But if the *Politico* stories are to be believed, the president's "old-fashioned" documents aren't safe either. *Politico* reported that Trump was ripping up official papers as soon as he was finished with them. Staff members started collecting the fragments from the Oval Office and other work spaces and sending them to records management staff, who taped the pieces of paper together by hand so that they could be sent to NARA for safekeeping. Then, *Politico* noted, two of those records managers were terminated by the White House, apparently without warning and without cause.[2]

In reality, the president doesn't seem to have much respect for the authenticity of evidence, no matter its shape or form. As recounted in the Mueller report, in February 2018, Trump ordered White House Counsel Don McGahn to write a letter stating that the president had never directed McGahn to fire the special counsel, even though other evidence suggests that Trump did indeed ask McGahn to fire Mueller. White House Secretary Robert Porter recalled Trump saying "something to the effect of 'If he doesn't write a letter, then maybe I'll have to get rid of him.'" When Trump and McGahn met to discuss the matter, Trump criticized McGahn for keeping records of the conversation. Trump challenged McGahn: "What about these notes? Why do you take notes? Lawyers don't take notes. I never had a lawyer who took notes."[3]

Trustworthy evidence does not just happen. There is no guarantee that any agency or person will make a "good" record, store it safely, or keep it for as long as needed. There is, consequently, no assurance that evidence will be available for those who may need it, now or later, whether their goal is to uphold rights, protect justice, seek connections, or share their memories. No one *has* to take notes. But in a democratic, rules-based society, surely it is reasonable to expect, as required by laws such as the Presidential Records Act, that presidents and government officials will provide documentary evidence of their actions and decisions. In reality, though, no society can legislate memory keeping, just as no society can legislate morality. The law can say, "Keep a record," but that record might just be one or two words on a sheet of paper: "Action taken" or "Decision made." We cannot rely on laws, and we cannot depend on technology. Instead, we have to change our understanding of evidence, shedding some outdated assumptions along the way.

Assuming Evidence Laws Are Adequate

One of the first assertions that the public had a right to evidence came in 1789, when the French Republic wrote its *Déclaration des droits de l'homme et du citoyen* (*Declaration of the Rights of the Man and of the Citizen*). Article 15 stated that "society has the right to ask a public official for an accounting of his administration." Back in the days of bishops and kings, being allowed to ask your government official to explain himself was revolutionary indeed.[4] Today there are multitudes of recordkeeping laws. The US Federal Records Act, for instance, requires that government departments establish records management programs and cooperate with NARA to preserve valuable evidence. And under the US criminal code, government employees can be fined for the intentional "concealment, removal, or mutilation of records."[5]

Underlying all this legislation is the principle of the rule of law: the concept that no one person is above the law. Ever since 1215, when England's King John was slapped down by his barons in Runnymeade and the *Magna Carta* was first crafted, democratic societies around the world have accepted that people must be held to account for their actions. And holding someone to account requires evidence. As clause 38 of the *Magna Carta* states, no one is to "put anyone to law by his accusation alone, without trustworthy witnesses being brought in for this." No proof; no prosecution.[6]

It is one thing to have a law, but what happens when governments ignore it? In October 2018, CREW, or Citizens for Responsibility and Ethics in Washington, sued the Department of Homeland Security and DHS Secretary Kirstjen Nielsen, arguing they had violated the Federal Records Act by failing to create adequate records of immigrant parents and children. After adopting a "zero tolerance policy" regarding asylum seekers in April 2018, US government officials began stopping illegal immigrants who arrived at the border as a family group. If a family arrived at the border without a visa, the family members were charged with criminal entry. The children were then removed from their parents' custody and placed in detention centers, shelters, or foster homes, while the parents were jailed or deported.[7]

In its lawsuit, CREW argued that the government's "haphazard" approach to recordkeeping had "catastrophic" consequences on the lives of the immigrants affected, adding that "rarely, if ever, has an agency's violation of its statutory recordkeeping obligations had such grave implications."[8] Indeed, if news reports are to be believed, border officials did not consistently manage the evidence needed to reconnect parents and children after they had been separated. To reunite families, government officials have apparently been forced to sort through paper copies of immigrant records to try to match children and parents, if they can find the parents at all.[9]

The recordkeeping weaknesses in the Department of Homeland Security will have deep repercussions on children and families for decades to come. Laws governing the creation and protection of evidence are not adequate, and more importantly, they do not come with significant consequences. What is the risk to breaking such laws when the punishment is only a slap on the wrist?

One of the problems with evidence laws is that they rarely clarify the difference between data, information, and evidence. A law might refer to "data" when it means "information" or "information" when it means "record." A reference to "record" in one law may really mean "evidence," but "evidence" might be defined in another law only in relation to admissibility in court. But when people use access to information laws, they are seeking evidence, not information. They want proof, not conjecture. And as the Facebook/Cambridge Analytica debacle in the United Kingdom illustrates, data that seem isolated and unidentified can actually be used as proof. A personal phone number or a Facebook "like" can be used as proof if it can be linked back to an individual. Similarly, CCTV footage, GPS location data, and DNA analysis can prove where someone was and what that someone was doing at a particular time and place. Data? Yes. Information? Yes. Evidence? Quite possibly. Our laws need to reflect the reality that seemingly transient and supposedly anonymous data have become proof.

Assuming Access and Privacy Are Guaranteed

Of course, legislating the protection of evidence does not mean that people have the right of access. The French declaration notwithstanding, access to evidence was rare until the middle of the 20th century. The research "public" was defined as accredited scholars, allowed to use only 20-, 50-, or 100-year-old historical archives. Contemporary evidence was rarely made available to the general populace. Now access to information laws are in place around the world, but many of them are in desperate need of modernization.

Canada's access legislation, for instance, has not been updated substantially since it was first passed in 1983. According to the 2018 Global Right to Information Rating, Canada slipped six places in the 2018 rankings, now sitting at the 56th spot, in large part because of its "antiquated approach to access to information." The United States ranks even lower, at 69th, far below countries such as Mexico, ranked 2nd, India, 6th, or South Africa, 14th.[10]

The 2001 USA PATRIOT Act, which gave the US government significant powers to access and use personal communications, expired in 2015, but subsequent laws have maintained the government's right to access personal information and evidence. The E-mail Privacy Act, brought forward in 2013 to replace the 1986 Electronic Communications Privacy Act, aimed to restrict government access to personal emails and other digital communications. As of April 2019, the act was still not law.[11]

The European Union's General Data Protection Regulation, or GDPR, which came into effect in May 2018, is the most robust privacy legislation in existence today. The GDPR requires that any person or organization that gathers, holds, or uses personal information about EU residents must protect each person's privacy at all times. *At all times.* The regulation applies not just to government offices or public agencies but to any agency that receives and uses personal data about someone, whether or not that agency is based in the European Union. If the person whose personal information is at issue is based in the European Union, that person's privacy rights must be respected, even if the information itself is physically stored outside of the European Union. In keeping with GDPR requirements, Google was fined €50 million (about US$57 million) in

January 2019 for not adequately disclosing to users how it was using personal data (evidence) collected across its various apps and services. Assuming the fine is not overturned, one can argue that GDPR is one of the first pieces of evidence legislation with such hefty penalties. (Ever wonder why, as you were shopping online or using social media in recent months, you began receiving so many notices requiring you formally to authorize access to your personal data? You can thank GDPR. Many businesses are actively obtaining permission now, before they collect any personal information, in order to get on the right side of a law that might not even apply to them.)[12]

Assuming Evidence Exists

While many laws require that officials make evidence available if it exists, few laws demand that agencies *make* good records in the first place.[13] Some argue it is asking too much to require the creation of "good" records of "important" actions or decisions. They say that requiring public agencies to record their decisions just adds unnecessary layers of bureaucracy. Others fear that departments will just wiggle around the law by conducting their business by telephone, storing their emails on personal servers instead of in official record-keeping systems, or writing cryptic messages saying "decision agreed" instead of documenting their actions fully and completely.

Certainly, agencies will try to skirt the law—always have, always will. In October 2017, the Japanese manufacturer Kobe Steel admitted that it had altered inspection certificates on aluminum and copper products to make it look like the products had met manufacturing requirements. The purpose of the deception, it seems, was to demonstrate that despite their light weight, the materials were still strong enough to use in the manufacture of cars, trains, or airplanes. Kobe seemed to believe that false evidence was necessary to secure market advantage.[14]

Also in Japan, it was reported in 2018 that the Japanese government had deliberately obscured the titles of hundreds of thousands of official documents. The goal was to make it harder for the public to access records under the country's freedom of information laws. As one former government official noted, "We were afraid that if the contents of documents could be easily assumed from their file names, it would be easier for members of the public to request disclosure of the documents. We feared that we would be a target of criticism based on the information that was disclosed." The vague and misleading file titles used included generic words such as "miscellaneous" and "documents concerning a conference." In the wake of the scandal, the former head of the Records Man-

agement Society of Japan publicly urged government officials to be more transparent, instead of preventing people from exercising their "right to know."[15]

Those who are accountable to the public should be required to produce
authentic evidence, and it seems eminently reasonable that they should be
penalized for failing to do so. There ought to be a central role for the recordkeeper in this process. As argued by Elizabeth Denham, the United Kingdom's
Information Commissioner,

> A great deal of the work of any FOI [freedom of information] regulator
> implicates the management of records and information, and this is becom-
> ing an ever more prominent part of our work. . . . Questions relating to the
> creation, proper management and maintenance of government records
> are therefore at the heart of what my office does. If public authorities do
> not maintain a proper record of their decisions and actions, if they do not
> properly manage their records, the public's right to gain access to informa-
> tion will be damaged, even thwarted.[16]

Assuming Evidence Is Safe

Another dangerous assumption is that once evidence makes its way into some
form of repository—physical or digital—it is safe. Nothing more need be done;
it is securely stored away, ever to remain thus, until someone wants to see it.
That assumption was shattered in September 2018, when fire consumed the
200-year-old National Museum of Brazil in Rio de Janeiro. In a matter of hours,
over 20 million items, from archaeological artifacts to archival documents,
along with thousands of hours of audiovisual recordings of indigenous languages, were incinerated. As journalists later discovered, the museum's physical facilities were crumbling. There was no facility-wide fire suppression system, and there was not enough water in nearby fire hydrants to extinguish the
flames. Firefighters had to draw water from a nearby lake.

After the fire, Marcelo Weksler, one of the curators at the museum, lamented
that "we knew that the fire one day was bound to happen. . . . It was our worst
nightmare."[17] Apparently, the Brazilian government did not consider museum
funding a priority. The museum's director, Alexander Kellner, noted that
museum officials had asked Brazil's National Development Bank for a loan
to improve the museum's infrastructure in 2015; negotiations continued for
almost three years without success. As Kellner complained, while the government was investing the equivalent of US$540 million in renovations to Rio's
soccer stadium in anticipation of the 2014 World Cup, the museum had to set

up a crowdfunding site to solicit funds to rebuild the base holding a dinosaur skeleton. The campaign raised $7,000.[18]

It is difficult to believe that the Brazilian government felt confident that the nation's artifacts, archaeological specimens, archives, historical publications, and audiovisual materials were safe in a 200-year-old wooden building with little to nothing in the way of environmental protection or security controls. The situation at the museum was so grave that museum officials did not even know what they had on display. After the disaster, they had to ask the public to share personal photographs taken during visits to the museum so that staff could piece together a picture of physical spaces and compile an inventory of what had been lost.[19]

Some may argue the situation in Brazil was an anomaly. Most custodial institutions, they believe, are equipped with strong storage facilities and adequate fire suppression systems. They are well staffed and adequately funded. Yes? No. In the cultural arena, which is already under-resourced, archives are the poor cousin to museums, libraries, and galleries. In 2014, the Council of State Archivists prepared an issue brief on the need for archival funding. It noted that in 2012 the Institute for Museum and Library Services provided $189 million to libraries across the nation, or about 60 cents per person. The institute provided another $30 million to support museums, or about 9 cents per person. The comparable federal agency representing archival interests, the National Historical Publications and Records Commission, provided about $2.5 million to support state and local archival operations across the country, or about 0.015 cents per person. One-tenth of one cent per person, to support the preservation of irreplaceable sources of evidence.[20]

Assuming Technology Is Stable

Ironically, though, and perhaps counterintuitively, it is often easier to ensure physical evidence is safe than to protect digital evidence. In 2018, the town of Litchfield, Connecticut, suffered a crisis with its digital records after the town experienced difficulties upgrading its computer operating systems. It wasn't until those problems were resolved, months later, that the town realized the new server hardware was flawed and, worse, that its backup systems were not running properly. Staff had to reenter manually information from paper records such as receipts, building permits, and vehicle registration documents. Luckily, the government hadn't destroyed the source evidence. Steve Ochmanski, who helps manage the town's computers, said that "until something like this happens, people don't think it's that important."[21]

In another case, news broke in August 2018 of a computer crash at Memorial University in St. John's, Newfoundland, and Labrador, Canada. The failure occurred during routine maintenance, when repair staff cut the electricity to the building and the backup power system collapsed. The backup to the backup provided about 40 minutes of power, but that was not enough to recover the material on the servers, which included about 70 terabytes of digital copies of archival documents, photographs, and newspapers. The university hoped to have the data restored within a month or two after the incident, but in the meantime, the university directed people to the "physical backups"—meaning the original paper records—which were still in storage on campus. What is going to happen when all the evidence we create is born digital and there are no physical backups?[22]

On April 15, 2018, the day the Internal Revenue Service requires all Americans to file their tax returns, the IRS's computer systems crashed. Apparently, they failed because the new (18-month-old) hardware had been installed on top of components that were up to 60 years old. The government had approved the upgrade but had not allocated enough funding to carry out the work quickly enough to ensure the transition was complete before the April rush. As David Power, the director of information technology management issues for the Government Accountability Office, said, a systems failure this huge was "was our biggest fear." But, he added, the systems were not down for a long time, so "we dodged a bullet."[23] How many bullets are we going to have to dodge before we invest in a sturdier bulletproof vest?

Recordkeepers have long recognized the fallibility of digital technologies. A website that existed on Monday might be gone on Tuesday. How can we maintain accountability if the evidence appears and disappears within a matter of hours? To mitigate this risk, the founder of the Internet Archive, Brewster Kahle, began capturing web pages in his "Wayback Machine" as early as 1996 in order to preserve source evidence that would otherwise be lost. The Internet Archive also preserves digital copies of books, audio recordings, videos, images, and software programs. As of 2018, the archive held nearly 300 billion web pages, 11 million books and texts, 4 million audio recordings (including 160,000 live concerts), 3 million videos, 1 million images, and 100,000 software programs.[24]

The Internet Archive is a noble institution, and its staff and volunteers offer a phenomenal service. But recordkeeping professionals like me find it terribly depressing to know that there is more secure documentary evidence in the repository of a nonprofit agency, which relies on grants and donations to support its work, than in the holdings of some of the oldest and largest publicly funded repositories in the world. It is time for the public to demand more of our governments: better laws, stricter controls, and better resources for the preservation of evidence, paper and digital. If we keep thinking of evidence as old, physical, and safe, we will not focus our attention on the essential job of protecting today's increasingly ephemeral digital evidence, which must be protected from the moment it is created.

Assuming the Future Is Digital

The battle to preserve trustworthy evidence is never ending. Yet, despite countless examples of crashed systems and lost data, it is too common for the average person, and the average government official, to assume that computer technologies will work the first time every time, and that any "information" problem can be solved by technology. The US government has put enough faith in the future of technology that starting in 2019, all permanent records produced by federal agencies will have to be electronic. No more paper. (The paperless office. Talk about a documentary nirvana.)[25]

Canada's Chief Information Officer, Alex Benay, argues that digital technologies can transform public service, if they are implemented well. As he says, a digital organization can respond effectively and rapidly to changing needs, reducing costs and risks and making organizations more efficient. Benay suggests that effective digital leaders will "embrace the chaos" and "be prepared to fail." Small failures and agile, flexible implementation programs are probably within accepted tolerance levels for most democracies. What happens, though, if individual failures turn into systematic breakdowns in infrastructure? Does a government have the right to risk accountability by taking a high-risk approach to evidence management? How much chaos can a government accept when the rights of its citizens are at stake?[26]

The newest innovation for accountable recordkeeping is blockchain technology, which was first developed to manage digital currencies such as bitcoin. The theory behind blockchain is that evidence can be divided into pieces, or blocks, which can then be encrypted. Each block can be linked together with hashes or codes, allowing blockchain users to see if any piece is missing. It is an exciting concept. But like other technologies through the centuries, there is never a guarantee that today's innovation will be sustainable. We must always be thinking about the downside as well as the upside, which is why, however exciting blockchain may be, it should not be seen as the ideal solution to such a complex problem as evidence management.

We also need to think more carefully about the impact of information technologies, not just on evidence but also on our economies, on our social and political systems, and on our environment. The Facebook/Cambridge Analytica fiasco in the United Kingdom and the recognition of foreign interference in US elections highlight the fact that companies like Facebook (valued at $140 billion), Google ($100 billion), and Apple (nearly $1 trillion) are not public utilities, any more than banks are public services, a lesson learned after the banking collapse of 2007–2008. Should we continue with this unregulated, uncontrolled approach to the management of our communications, data, and evidence? Do we want to keep living in this digital Wild West? If we are going to immerse ourselves so fully in a digital world, perhaps we need to establish some reasonable boundaries.

For instance, should social media providers be able to make our personal evidence—including data and information that can be linked back to us—available to third-party companies without our express permission? Should computer companies push customers to keep "upgrading" digital devices that are still perfectly usable, while placing our evidence at risk in the process? Should Internet service providers be able to block or slow down the delivery of Internet traffic to customers who do not pay for premium connection services? I say no to all of the above.

Societies regulate the activities of health care providers, power utilities, and construction companies. Why shouldn't they impose a comparable measure of control over digital technologies and service providers? The State of California has taken a major step forward, implementing digital privacy laws comparable to the GDPR. The state has also passed a law to ensure net neutrality, prohibiting companies like AT&T or Comcast from blocking Internet traffic in order to control competition. One can only hope that other states follow suit, and that the federal government takes a leadership role in protecting citizens' rights by providing stronger oversight over the management of digital data and evidence.[27]

As Apple CEO Tim Cook said in October 2018, the gap in privacy protection alone "isn't just wrong, it is destructive." The gap is not just in privacy, though. There is an economic gap—growing into an abyss—between those who can afford to access new technologies and those who are left behind. How equitable will our society be if everyone must depend on digital technologies to access critical evidence such as medical or social service records, financial documents, or legal or property records? What happens to those who cannot afford to have a computer at home, or those who do not even have a home?[28]

Digital pioneer Tim Berners-Lee, the inventor of the World Wide Web, has questioned the sustainability of our current relationship with information technologies. Disillusioned by the Web, Berners-Lee is developing a new, decentralized platform called Solid, which will run on top of the existing Web. His goal is to return control of data to users by breaking up the centralized control that now dominates the Internet space. As Berners-Lee argues, we have reached a "critical tipping point." The Web, he notes, "has evolved into an engine of inequity and division; swayed by powerful forces who use it for their own agendas."[29]

And what about the environmental impact of digital technology? As we expand our digital footprint—or fingerprints?—we are becoming deeply, inextricably dependent on electricity. But access to power is not a given. We need to think carefully about whether and how we can guarantee continued access to information and evidence when our power systems fail, as they can and do. As cultural anthropologist Gretchen Bakke argues, the grid is not a technological system. "It is," she writes, "also a legal one, a business one, a political one, a cultural one, and a weather-driven one, and the ebbs and flows in each domain affect the very possibility of success." How many evidential eggs are we placing in the basket of power lines and electrical grids?[30]

A quarter century ago the Canadian archivist Terry Cook argued that we face the dichotomy of "electronic records, paper minds." We still do. We cannot continue to manage the products of digital technologies effectively if we don't completely reimagine how evidence can be created, managed, and protected.[31] To make this change, we need to shed our assumption: that our laws are adequate, that our evidence is safe, that technology is stable, or that the digital future is secure. We need to bridge the gap. Technology is not the answer; it is the reality. As automation gets smaller, faster, and cheaper, we are only just starting to realize the enormous infrastructure, economic, and environmental impacts computers have on our lives. But in these dangerous times for truth and facts, not having trustworthy evidence is *not* an option. We must change course.

NOTES

1. The Presidential Records Act can be seen at https://www.archives.gov/about/laws/presidential-records.html, *archived at* https://perma.cc/DTG3-6Z35.

2. See the news story by Josh Dawsey and Bryan Bender, "National Archives Warned Trump White House to Preserve Documents," *Politico*, October 17, 2017, https://www.politico.com/story/2017/10/17/national-archives-trump-documents-preserve-243888, *archived at* https://perma.cc/3E9Q-4KH3. See also Annie Karni, "Meet the Guys Who Tape Trump's Papers Back Together," *Politico*, June 10, 2018, https://www.politico.com/story/2018/06/10/trump-papers-filing-system-635164, *archived*

at https://perma.cc/Z653-UQLZ; and Associated Press, "Trump Says He Doesn't Trust Computers as He Rings in 2017," *Fortune*, January 1, 2017, http://fortune .com/2017/01/01/trump-doesnt-trust-computers, *archived at* https://perma.cc/ C6K4-VVPA.

3. Special Counsel Robert S. Mueller III, *Report on the Investigation into Russian Interference in the 2016 Presidential Election* (Washington, DC: US Department of Justice, March 2019), vol. II, esp. 115–17, https://www.justice.gov/sco, *archived at* https://perma.cc/LQY3-MPVG, as published by *The New York Times* at https://www .nytimes.com/interactive/2019/04/18/us/politics/mueller-report-document.html, *archived at* https://perma.cc/GHN7-2AYF. Porter left his position only days after this exchange took place, after he was accused of domestic abuse, and McGahn resigned in October 2018—pushed out, many have argued, because he would not accede to Trump's demands. The revolving door of government appointments under Trump's presidency, including Porter and McGahn, has been tracked by many journalists, including Denise Lu and Karen Yourish, "The Turnover at the Top of the Trump Administration," *The New York Times*, April 12, 2019, https://www.nytimes .com/interactive/2018/03/16/us/politics/all-the-major-firings-and-resignations -in-trump-administration.html, *archived at* https://perma.cc/MP6D-AUTA.

4. An English translation of the French declaration can be seen at http://www .conseil-constitutionnel.fr/conseil-constitutionnel/root/bank_mm/anglais/cst 2.pdf, *archived at* https://perma.cc/9TCE-MUWJ. Note that the English translation of the declaration's title and contents has varied across different sources in the two centuries since the declaration was first written.

5. Records-related legislation can be seen on the NARA website at https://www .archives.gov/about/laws, *archived at* https://perma.cc/B59M-VK53. Section 2107 of the NARA legislation (44 U.S.C. chap. 21) covers the acceptance of records for preservation. The criminal code (see, esp., 18 U.S.C. pt. 1, chap. 101, sec. 2071) can be accessed on the US Government Publishing Office website at https://www.gpo .gov/fdsys/browse/collectionUScode.action?collectionCode=USCODE, *archived at* https://perma.cc/5UQ2-5RNK.

6. The general concept of the rule of law had been recognized as far back as ancient Greece, as well as in Rome, China, and India, but the *Magna Carta* is often held up in Western society as the most forceful statement of the principle. It does make a great story, with a moustache-twirling villain in King John. But Tom Bingham's *Rule of Law* (New York: Penguin, 2011) provides a much more thorough account of the history of the concept and its application over time. Also informative is the discussion of the rule of law in United Nations, *The Rule of Law and Transitional Justice in Conflict and Post-Conflict Societies: Report of the Secretary-General* (United Nations Security Council, August 23, 2004), https://www.un.org/ruleoflaw/ what-is-the-rule-of-law, *archived at* https://perma.cc/Y38R-MDZM.

7. CREW, "CREW Sues DHS for Child Separation Recordkeeping Failures" (press release, October 26, 2018), https://www.citizensforethics.org/press-release/ crew-sues-dhs-for-child-separation-recordkeeping-failures, *archived at* https:// perma.cc/HEC3-KB5Y. See also Katherine Hawkins, "Just Following Orders: Overdue Oversight and Unanswered Questions on Family Separations," POGO

.org, "Oversight: Analysis," August 8, 2018, http://www.pogo.org/blog/2018/08/just-following-orders-overdue-oversight-and-unanswered-questions-on-family-separation.html, *archived at* https://perma.cc/4XPE-ARYT.

8. CREW, "CREW Sues DHS." See also Hawkins, "Just Following Orders."

9. See Caitlin Dickerson, "Trump Administration in Chaotic Scramble to Reunify Migrant Families," *The New York Times*, July 5, 2018, https://www.nytimes.com/2018/07/05/us/migrant-children-chaos-family-separation.html, *archived at* https://perma.cc/KZ4M-9HQ3. See also Ron Nixon, "'Lost' Immigrant Children? That's a Different Story," *The New York Times*, May 31, 2018, https://www.nytimes.com/2018/05/31/insider/lost-immigrant-children-article.html, *archived at* https://perma.cc/T5N6-ZHXQ. It is unclear if the resignation of DHS Secretary Kirstjen Nielsen on April 7, 2019, will affect the status of the lawsuit. For background on Nielsen's resignation, see Zolan Kanno-Youngs, Maggie Haberman, Michael D. Shear, and Eric Schmitt, "Kirstjen Nielsen Resigns as Trump's Homeland Security Secretary," *The New York Times*, April 7, 2019, https://www.nytimes.com/2019/04/07/us/politics/kirstjen-nielsen-dhs-resigns.html?login=email&auth=login-email, *archived at* https://perma.cc/2JQH-VXR8.

10. The annual Global Right to Information ratings are compiled by the Canadian-based Centre for Law and Democracy and the European-based Access Info. See Anna Desmarais, "Canada's Freedom of Information Laws 'Very Outdated': Commissioner," *iPolitics*, September 28, 2018, https://ipolitics.ca/2018/09/28/canadas-freedom-of-information-laws-very-outdated-commissioner, *archived at* https://perma.cc/6Y2K-DU2B.

11. See David Ruiz, "Email Privacy Act Comes Back, Hopefully to Stay," Electronic Frontier Foundation, *DeepLinks* (blog), May 29, 2018, https://www.eff.org/deeplinks/2018/05/email-privacy-act-comes-back-hopefully-stay, *archived at* https://perma.cc/6CRC-4E6H.

12. For details of the Google fine, see Adam Satariano, "Google Is Fined $57 Million Under Europe's Data Privacy Law," *The New York Times*, January 21, 2019, available at https://www.nytimes.com/2019/01/21/technology/google-europe-gdpr-fine.html, *archived at* https://perma.cc/GT56-WPU3. It is true that the GDPR offers strict controls to protect privacy, but some would suggest that the pendulum has swung too far. In an effort to address growing calls for the "right to be forgotten," the GDPR allows a person to request that personal data be erased from digital sources, such as databases or Google search results, if the person believes the information is inaccurate or is no longer needed for the intended purpose. Those in favor of erasing digital evidence argue that a person's quality of life should not be diminished because false or hostile news stories are "out there," particularly if the information is not correct. One could counter, however, that a printed newspaper story might also reflect information that changes later: Does this mean we should destroy old newspapers if we don't like the content? On the other hand, there is a back door to these and other GDPR requirements. According to Article 89, data can be preserved "for archiving purposes in the public interest" or for scientific, historical research, or statistical purposes. Recordkeeping professionals face a major challenge as they attempt

to pick apart this Gordian knot of access versus privacy. For more on the GDPR, see the European Commission's website at https://ec.europa.eu/commission/priorities/justice-and-fundamental-rights/data-protection/2018-reform-eu-data-protection-rules_en, *archived at* https://perma.cc/BQ72-F83S, and the European Union's GDPR portal at https://eugdpr.org, *archived at* https://perma.cc/X6WS-7NMJ.

13. One exception is financial evidence, which is often more tightly controlled than are other types of evidence. Article 1, section 9 of the US Constitution explicitly requires that "no Money shall be drawn from the Treasury, but in Consequence of Appropriations made by Law; and a regular Statement and Account of the Receipts and Expenditures of all public Money shall be published from time to time." Canadian archivist Richard Valpy analyzes the strength of financial laws and regulations in Canada to make a compelling case for a similarly robust legislative framework for other government records; see his article "For the Purpose of Accountability—The Need for a Comprehensive Recordkeeping Act," *Archivaria* 88 (forthcoming).

14. See Jonathan Soble and Neal E. Boudette, "Kobe Steel's Falsified Data Is Another Blow to Japan's Reputation," *The New York Times*, October 10, 2017, https://www.nytimes.com/2017/10/10/business/kobe-steel-japan.html, *archived at* https://perma.cc/WL5N-5AAQ.

15. The story was published in Japanese and English by *The Mainichi* newspaper, under the title "'Deliberately' Obscure Gov't File Names Leave Japan's National Archives at a Loss," August 6, 2018, https://mainichi.jp/english/articles/20180806/p2a/00m/0na/030000c, *archived at* https://perma.cc/8MVE-V8UK.

16. See the text of Denham's speech, "Trust, Transparency and Just-in-Time FOI: Sustainable Governance and Openness in the Digital Age" (University College London, March 22, 2018), at https://ico.org.uk/about-the-ico/news-and-events/news-and-blogs/2018/03/trust-transparency-and-just-in-time-foi-sustainable-governance-and-openness-in-the-digital-age, *archived at* https://perma.cc/X4VD-5RFP.

17. See Manuela Andreoni, "Museum Fire in Brazil Was 'Bound to Happen,'" *The New York Times*, September 4, 2018, https://www.nytimes.com/2018/09/04/world/americas/brazil-museum-fire.html?action=click&module=RelatedLinks&pgtype=Article, *archived at* https://perma.cc/V8TK-23SA.

18. See Ana Rita Cunha and Judite Cypreste, "Relatos de falta de verba e abandono do Museu Nacional remontam à década de 1950," *Aos Fatos*, September 3, 2018, https://aosfatos.org/noticias/relatos-de-falta-de-verba-e-abandono-do-museu-nacional-remontam-decada-de-1950, *archived at* https://perma.cc/K3E7-JUD8. For Kellner's remarks, see Andreoni, "Museum Fire in Brazil." See also the transcript of Ari Shapiro, "Anthropologist Mourns Loss of His Work and History from Museum Fire in Brazil," NPR's *All Things Considered*, September 4, 2018, https://www.npr.org/2018/09/04/644618102/anthropologist-mourns-loss-of-his-work-and-history-from-museum-fire-in-brazil, *archived at* https://perma.cc/B5MZ-Z9AM. See also Associated Press, "Firefighters Going through Burned-Out National Museum," *AP News*, September 3, 2018, https://www.apnews.com/

777339758e6e461bb1238945872ca4ee, *archived at* https://perma.cc/VZQ2
-HSU3.

19. See Lela Moore, "Fire Devastated the National Museum of Brazil: Show Us
    What Was Lost," *The New York Times*, September 6, 2018, https://www.nytimes
    .com/2018/09/06/reader-center/national-museum-of-brazil-photos.html?action
    =click&module=RelatedCoverage&pgtype=Article&region=Footer, *archived at*
    https://perma.cc/J3AN-DW5E.

20. See Council of State Archivists, "Issue Brief: Adequate Funding of Government
    Archives and Archival Programs" (CoSA, 2014), https://www.statearchivists.org/
    programs/advocacy/issue-briefs-position-statements, *archived at* https://perma
    .cc/MS52-9SZQ.

21. Charles Eichacker, "Litchfield's Town Computer System Endures 'A Perfect Storm'
    of Failures," *Kennebec Journal*, September 2, 2018, https://www.pressherald.com/
    2018/09/02/litchfields-town-computer-system-endures-a-perfect-storm-of
    -failures, *archived at* https://perma.cc/49RY-57HG.

22. "Server Crash Takes Out Rich Digital Archive at Memorial University," *CBC News*,
    August 16, 2018, https://www.cbc.ca/news/canada/newfoundland-labrador/
    mun-digital-archives-wiped-out-1.4787960, *archived at* https://perma.cc/3HMT
    -XT6D.

23. Aaron Boyd and Frank Konkel, "IRS' 60-Year-Old IT System Failed on Tax Day
    Due to New Hardware," *Nextgov*, April 19, 2018, https://www.nextgov.com/
    it-modernization/2018/04/irs-60-year-old-it-system-failed-tax-day-due-new
    -hardware/147598, *archived at* https://perma.cc/TN3B-NJGC.

24. For more on the Internet Archive, see https://archive.org/about, *archived at*
    https://perma.cc/9NKH-EQHH.

25. Adam Mazmanian, "National Archives Tilts toward Paperless Future," *FCW*,
    August 24, 2017, https://fcw.com/articles/2017/08/24/nara-paperless-future
    -mazmanian.aspx, *archived at* https://perma.cc/NB7E-HQS9. For details about
    NARA's process for deciding which records are kept permanently, see chapter 5 of
    NARA's guide, *Disposition of Federal Records: A Records Management Handbook*
    (2000 Web Edition, currently under revision), https://www.archives.gov/records-
    mgmt/publications/disposition
    -of-federal-records, *archived at* https://perma.cc/V2S2-J9QL. See also Jason
    Barron, *The Impact of NARA's Email Capstone Policy and Other Recent Initiatives
    on FOIA Access* (Freedom of Information Act Advisory Committee, October 19,
    2017), https://www.archives.gov/files/Baron-foia-advisory-committee-presentation
    .pdf, *archived at* https://perma.cc/TMV3-V33A; and NARA, *White Paper on the
    Capstone Approach and Capstone GRS* (April 2015), https://www.archives.gov/
    files/records-mgmt/email-management/final-capstone-white-paper.pdf, *archived
    at* https://perma.cc/LV7W-6LQM.

26. Alex Benay, *Government Digital: The Quest to Regain Public Trust* (Toronto:
    Dundurn, 2018): e-book loc. 1362–97.

27. The new California legislation is discussed in a Taft Stettinius & Hollister LLP
    article, "Change Is in the California Air as Legislature Amends New Privacy Law,"

in *Lexology*, October 22, 2018, https://www.lexology.com/library/detail.aspx?g=27d07b1d-7fcb-433d-a897-377fc6cb2dfb, *archived at* https://perma.cc/2GX5-BJED. Background information can be found at Dipayan Ghosh, "What You Need to Know about California's New Data Privacy Law," *Harvard Business Review*, July 11, 2018, https://hbr.org/2018/07/what-you-need-to-know-about-californias-new-data-privacy-law, *archived at* https://perma.cc/Q9UV-X5LV. The net neutrality law is discussed in Heather Kelly, "California Just Passed Its Net Neutrality Law: The DOJ Is Already Suing," *CNN Business*, October 1, 2018, https://www.cnn.com/2018/10/01/tech/california-net-neutrality-law/index.html, *archived at* https://perma.cc/3AV4-J6DY.

28. Cook's speech and analysis of his comments can be found at Sara Salinas and Sam Meredith, "Tim Cook: Personal Data Collection Is Being 'Weaponized against Us with Military Efficiency,'" *CNBC Tech*, October 25, 2018, https://www.cnbc.com/2018/10/24/apples-tim-cook-warns-silicon-valley-it-would-be-destructive-to-block-strong-privacy-laws.html, *archived at* https://perma.cc/EZK4-QZ5K. See also Tony Romm, "Apple's Tim Cook Blasts Silicon Valley Over Privacy Issues," *The Washington Post*, October 24, 2018, https://www.washingtonpost.com/world/europe/apples-tim-cook-delivers-searing-critique-of-silicon-valley/2018/10/24/5adaa586-d6dd-11e8-8384-bcc5492fef49_story.html?utm_term=.7c9aa3ad9d8e&wpisrc=nl_cybersecurity202&wpmm=1, *archived at* https://perma.cc/S36H-DCPF.

29. Isobel Asher Hamilton, "Tim Berners-Lee Launched His Vision for an Alternative Web, and His Timing Was Impeccable," *Business Insider*, October 1, 2018, https://www.businessinsider.com/tim-berners-lee-reveals-vision-alternative-web-solid-2018-10, *archived at* https://perma.cc/524L-GTPJ.

30. Gretchen Bakke, *The Grid: The Fraying Wires between Americans and Our Energy Future* (New York: Bloomsbury, 2016), 271. We—we the recordkeeping profession and we society at large—have not yet fully grasped the financial and environmental costs of digital dependency. How much does it really cost, in terms of physical space, electricity, heat, water, and light, never mind staff time, to preserve paper, analog, or digital archives? When people say, "Just digitize it all," they are perhaps not aware of some harsh realities. For instance, very often paper records will still need to be preserved, which means that while digitizing may make access easier, it will not necessarily reduce the overall costs of preserving those records in perpetuity. As well, the protection of both the digital and paper records requires continuous access to reliable sources of energy. If we embrace wholly digital archival operations, then we will become entirely dependent on persistent access to "the grid." Until we can guarantee that, are we really sure we want to scan everything and ditch the originals?

31. Terry Cook, "Electronic Records, Paper Minds: The Revolution in Information Management and Archives in the Post-Custodial and Post-Modernist Era," *Archives and Manuscripts* 22 (November 1994): 300–328.

10

"An arms race against the forces of fakery"

Evidence and Accountability

*If the people cannot trust their government to do
the job for which it exists—to protect them and to
promote their common welfare—all else is lost.*

Barack Obama, 2006

IN DECEMBER 2016, A TRIO OF RESEARCHERS AT THE UNIVERSITY OF
Toronto began what they called a "guerilla archiving" initiative, hosting a "hackathon" to capture and preserve copies of climate data stored on the website of
the US Environmental Protection Agency. The group feared that once he was in
office, incoming US President Donald Trump would delete evidence that con-
tradicted his arguments that global warming was a "hoax." Their efforts made
the American news, prompting comedian Stephen Colbert to joke, "It's gotten
so bad even *facts* are moving to Canada."[1]

The fear that the Trump administration would not protect authentic evidence has been realized many times over. Politicians have withheld the results
of environmental studies, removed evidence of climate change from official
websites, and edited official records to hide or diminish facts. Solid, verifiable
proof of the environmental impact of water contamination, overfishing, air
pollution, and carbon emissions has been altered or erased.[2]

The disregard for the environment is reprehensible, and the cavalier approach
to evidence is inexcusable. Recordkeeping professionals, whose underlying
tenet is to remain impartial protectors, not political actors, should not have to
become militant activists in order to ensure that sources of evidence are safe.

As we consider how to protect evidence, I believe we can learn something
from the effort to save our environment. Even though we still have a long way
to go, we have seen improvements in environmental legislation and regulations, which provides us with a model for improving the legislative framework

for evidence. We have developed more efficient, more environmentally sustainable technologies; we can learn from this work to devise tools and technologies that help protect trustworthy proof. We have raised awareness of the crisis facing Planet Earth, and we can do the same for evidence. We must change direction before it is too late.

Changing Course

When I was a child, people didn't think twice about tossing their waste in the landfill. Compost piles were for farmers, not city folk. Today, recycling containers are a common sight in my town, and children scold their parents for not placing their plastics or compost in the right bins. The phrase *Reduce, Reuse, Recycle* speaks volumes to us, as does the sentence at the bottom of our emails that reads, "Before printing, think of the environment." We still have a long way to go with environmental protection, but much has changed in half a century.[3]

We need to take evidence management just as seriously, and we need to act fast. Access to reliable and authentic sources of proof is critically important to democracy, human rights, and our sense of who we are and where we have come from. Without trustworthy evidence, we cannot ensure our governments respect the law and the rule of law, and we cannot hold them accountable for their actions and decisions—not just to a judge in a courtroom but to themselves, society, and posterity. Without evidence, we cannot hold *ourselves* accountable either. A life worth living *is* a life examined. Evidence helps us conduct that psychological and spiritual introspection with honesty and integrity.

What if we adopt a recordkeeping equivalent to *Reduce, Reuse, Recycle*? I propose *Remember, Respect, Record*. We need to *Remember*, with honesty, integrity, and clarity. Being able to remember our actions, decisions, and opinions—those we made this morning and those we made a decade ago—is essential to charting an evidence-based course of action. To remember well, we need to *Respect* the value of trustworthy evidence. We need to distinguish between information with only short-term value and evidence with long-term value. To remember and respect, we need to *Record* our actions, decisions, and opinions so that we have the authentic evidence we need to defend rights, support accountability, create identities, and preserve memories.

Recordkeeping professionals cannot achieve this change alone. Everyone needs to be involved, from information technology specialists and government policy makers to educators and the public. We all need to change our understanding of evidence, just as we have changed our understanding of waste. We are learning to segregate our valuable possessions from recyclable products and worthless objects, to reduce waste and protect our environment. Similarly, we need to look differently at data, information, and evidence, segregating and protecting valuable evidence and deleting obsolete information as a matter of course. We do a disservice to ourselves, our society, and our future by lumping it all together as "just" data.

What if government decision makers were required by law to create authentic proof of core decisions and actions consistently, not arbitrarily? What if chief information officers focused not on technology or information but on evidence? What if IT specialists designed digital storage systems that captured electronic records as official evidence, locking them down so they couldn't be changed later? What if educators incorporated raising awareness about evidence into the curriculum, whether for adults, teenagers, or kindergarteners? What if when people received emails, they saw a line of text at the bottom of each message that read, "Before deleting, think of the future." What marvelous changes these would be.

Strengthening the Law

Stronger legal and regulatory frameworks have helped to improve environmental management by reducing allowable fuel emissions or increasing the efficiency of waste management. Death rates from air pollution have fallen significantly in those parts of the world that have imposed stricter environmental controls.[4] Similarly, legislation and regulations can help improve the management of evidence. We need to revise existing laws, many of which were first developed in the predigital era, and we need to develop new laws to address the growing impact of technology.

Legislation should distinguish clearly between data, information, and evidence. When people file an access request, they are searching for evidence, not information. When they want their privacy protected, they are concerned about evidence, not information. Data protection is not about "raw" data; it is about any data that can be used as proof. This includes Facebook "likes," CCTV footage, GPS location data, and DNA analysis, all of which can be used to "prove" who someone is, where that person was, when, and even why. We need to ensure our evidence laws match the reality of our technologies.

We also need laws that ensure public officials, whether civil servants or politicians, are required to create authoritative and trustworthy evidence in the first place. Access to information legislation may require that an agency make available information (read: evidence) if it exists. But few laws demand that agencies regularly and consistently document their actions or decisions. We have learned that a corporation is more likely to adhere to environmental laws if it faces a $5 million penalty for noncompliance instead of a trifling $5,000 fine (the environmental equivalent of a traffic ticket). Similarly, evidence laws should outline reasonable recordkeeping requirements and punish lapses appropriately.[5]

Another regulatory change would be to demand that governments and businesses conduct evidence assessments, just as many are required to conduct environmental assessments now. If a manufacturer is going to build a new plant, it must document its efforts not to pollute. Why shouldn't it also have to prove that it will create, capture, and preserve authentic evidence of its operations? It should also be required to articulate its strategy for protecting privacy and making evidence available appropriately. Some jurisdictions already carry out privacy impact assessments, but those analyses identify only that portion of information and evidence that needs to be protected in order to secure someone's personal privacy. Few governments specifically define which records ought to be produced in the first place.

Even though we want governments to be as transparent as possible, we all know that sometimes secrets must be kept. Not everyone has the right to know the terms and conditions of a labor negotiation, the details of a person's medical condition, or the schematics of a nuclear power facility. As journalism professor Michael Schudson argues, even in an age of increased transparency, secrecy is not disappearing. "As our lives are more interconnected," he writes, "they are more visible to others in ways that serve us but also endanger us." Sometimes, he argues, it is inevitable and essential to keep secrets.[6]

In reality, most public servants do not want to deceive or dissemble. They are *public servants*, after all, and most of them want very much to uphold their statutory obligations and serve the public. The problem is that evidence management is not seen as an important part of their job. Records and data are often perceived as by-products; people don't tend to think much about how they are made, and they pay little attention to how they are protected. Someone else does that, they assume. But in a digital age, "someone else" might not get to the records in time to protect them before they are deleted or misfiled, whether by accident or design.

To create trustworthy evidence while respecting privacy and improving transparency, we have to look beyond legislation. We have to change workplace practices. New laws should not complicate government; they need to be accompanied by training and support for day-to-day recordkeeping. If office workers know that they must make authentic and accountable records, *and* if they are given the support they need to achieve that result, they will be much more successful—and much more satisfied.

Improving Technologies

We also need to improve the technologies we use to create data, information, and records, just as we have had to design better, cleaner, and more sustainable technologies to support environmental management. Recordkeeping professionals continuously work with software developers, computer experts, and information security specialists to develop more powerful and effective information technologies. For instance, we are actively developing and improving automated processes for the capture of metadata, descriptive information, and other contextual information about a record, allowing us to identify and manage valuable evidence more efficiently. We are also researching the potential for machine learning and artificial intelligence to help us identify and protect evidence while deleting obsolete data. And we are working to implement stronger security protocols to ensure that digital evidence cannot be hacked, leaked, stolen, or destroyed.

But recordkeepers are always gazing into the future, looking for an exit strategy even as we adopt the latest technology. In little more than a decade, for instance, we have watched the process for storing digital records move from burning a CD to backing up on a hard drive, then from hard drive storage to data tape storage, then from tape preservation to encryption using blockchain technologies. Perhaps the next move will be from blockchain to DNA coding. With technology, the only constant is change. We must stay ahead of the changes to ensure digital evidence is safe.

We also have to build technology that protects evidence by default. It wasn't that long ago that we all drove around in cars without seatbelts or air bags. But laws changed, technology changed, and lives were saved. We should be able to achieve the same with information technologies. We need to design systems that achieve "evidence by design" and "privacy by design." We can use artificial intelligence and machine learning more effectively to review and redact documents for access requests, saving time and effort. Recordkeepers are also helping to design tools and processes that create and capture records with confidential content segregated, to protect privacy while making it easier to release evidence quickly. Open government will truly be open when we change how we make evidence in the first place.

We also need to build technologies that capture and preserve authentic evidence the moment it is made, so it cannot be altered later. Companies such as Serelay in the United Kingdom are developing "trusted media capture" tools that can authenticate every bit and byte in a digital photograph or video. Roy Azoulay, founder and CEO of Serelay, says his goal is to find a way to ensure people can trust online content. "There's one of two roads," he argues. "One road is that we come to a place where we can't trust any video we see. . . . The second road is what we're hoping to find a solution for . . . making images and videos inherently verifiable." Machine learning and artificial intelligence can help authenticate originals, weed out duplicates, and highlight changes in evidence in ways no human could ever do.[7]

Still, we all need to temper our enthusiasm for each "latest and greatest" computer technology. We embraced the internal combustion engine, petroleum-based plastics, and tons and tons of packaging without really questioning the long-term consequences. We are paying the price now. I think we should adopt a more judicious approach to the tools we use to create and manage evidence, so we don't pay a similar price with lost or corrupted evidence. Computer programs are not stable. Digital storage is not cheap. Hardware is not infallible. Today's top-of-the-line computer might be tomorrow's Commodore 64.

Trying to rescue scattered pieces of evidence from IT systems after the fact is just as counterintuitive as cleaning up oceans of plastic instead of reducing our consumption in the first place. The public should demand better. We should reject any hardware or software that cannot guarantee that the content it holds, whether family photographs or nuclear launch codes, is authentic and safe. If we can't change laws or build new technologies by ourselves, at least we can flex our muscles in the marketplace.

Taking Personal Responsibility

We need to lobby for better laws, better oversight, and the appropriate use of technology. But we need to clean our own house too. We all need to take a hard look at how we create, manage, and preserve our own sources of evidence. Do we keep our back-up drive on the shelf next to our computer, in the same room? If there were a fire, all would be lost. Do we store our photographs on a raft of unlabeled USB keys tossed in a cupboard? How will anyone figure out what is worth keeping and what is junk if we aren't there to interpret? Do we store all our emails or documents in the cloud? How do we know the company holding those records adheres to best-practice storage and security protocols? How seriously does the average person take the protection of evidence if the most common passwords in the world are "123456" and "password"?[8]

As I noted earlier, Google has been fined for privacy violations under the GDPR. One of the services involved was Google Plus, which, it was discovered, had weak security systems, resulting in the potential disclosure of the private data (evidence) of up to 500,000 Google Plus users. Before news broke of the

GDPR fine, Google decided to shut down the Google Plus social media site, without letting people know of the breach.[9]

A hefty fine is certainly one form of punishment, but perhaps public censure would also be appropriate. We could all rise in protest that our privacy was violated and that because Google Plus is shutting down, through no fault of our own, we all have to take the time to clean up our Google Plus accounts and transfer our photographs, chats, and news feeds elsewhere. But I wonder, do some of us even remember that we have a Google Plus account? Surely we have a responsibility to pay much closer attention to the profusion of digital accounts we have established.

In 2018, the popular photo sharing site Flickr changed its terms and conditions, announcing it was going to start imposing a default storage limit. People could keep 1,000 photos on the site for free. After that, they would need to upgrade to a premium storage service. (The backstory seems to be that Flickr was taken over by Verizon and then by SmugMug, resulting in increased competition, at which time Flickr began looking for ways to increase revenues.) People protested the change in limits. "How are we going to get our thousands of other photographs out of one app and into another?" they cried. Some called it a case of corporate abandonment. What right did Flickr have, people argued, to deny them a service they had come to depend on so heavily?[10]

I am not sure the long-term storage of our photographs is entirely, or even largely, Flickr's problem. No form of evidence is consistently stable, and no storage system is entirely safe. Archival storage rooms burn down. Paper records get ruined in a flood. CDs and DVDs rot. Cloud storage systems can be hacked. Commercial service providers change their policies, restructure their services, or go out of business. As consumers, though, we seem far too comfortable putting our documents, photographs, and other sources of evidence in a variety of personal and commercial storage systems. It's like moving our eggs from one basket to another. The question is not which basket to use. The question is, do we really, really need thousands upon thousands of eggs? How many drafts of a document do we need? Which ones? Why? How many emails? Why? How many photographs? *Why?*

We all need to be more thoughtful about what evidence we want to keep. We should preserve the evidence that has enduring value and weed out the records and data that do not. Keep the best and delete the rest. But, you ask, what *is* worth keeping? Throughout this book, I have told stories of the kinds of evidence societies create, and how the records and data in those examples proved valuable: for justice and rights, identity and connections, memory and history. Consider your personal or business records in light of those stories:

What rights are protected by the evidence? What stories would not be told if you did not have the records? If you need help figuring out what to keep, ask an archivist. Helping you preserve your evidence is what we do.

Though I want everyone to be more attentive to how they create and manage their evidence, I don't want people to stop creating records. Far from it. I want us all to take photographs, keep diaries, write letters, and share stories. I want us to interview our grandparents, ask our uncles and aunts about their child-hoods, and identify the people in those photographs stored in the shoe boxes in the closet. We all have a role to play. We can and should preserve our valuable sources of recorded evidence, so that the world can know that we were here. As Ken Burns said, "Write: write letters. Keep journals. Besides your children, there is no surer way of achieving immortality."[11]

Raising Awareness

We have learned, perhaps too late, that in order to achieve significant environ-mental change, the public needs to speak out. We need to be equally vocal if we want to improve the management of evidence. We need to lobby for effec-tive and enforceable laws and for the development of accountable and efficient information technologies. We need to object, loudly and often, to the misuse, abuse, and neglect of evidence. We need to call out lies, alternative facts, and fake news. We need to demand equitable access to trustworthy proof. We need to regain our ethical bearings, rather than letting technology run amok. And we need to encourage evidence literacy, especially in the born-digital generation, who will be the decision makers of the future.

We the public, including recordkeepers speaking as concerned citizens, need to demand better from our governments and from the mass of corporations that increasingly control our lives. The people of Iceland protested the collapse of their banks, and they protested their government's failure to document important policy decisions and actions. The Pots and Pans Revolution led to significant legislative change in the creation and management of authentic evi-dence. Iceland's success offers a model for others to follow.

In April 2017, when people rallied in Washington, DC, in the March for Science, they were not just calling for the government to apply science-based policies and fund scientific research. They were also demanding that the gov-ernment demonstrate accountability and respect for evidence. Perhaps it is time for a March for Evidence? The public should demand that public officials recognize the difference between data, information, and evidence, insisting that the government implement policies and procedures that protect evidence, whatever its form. Only by creating, capturing, preserving, and making available authentic evidence will we start to see an end to the dizzying swirl of lies we face every day.[12]

We need to look at information, evidence, and technology not just with an eye to expedience but with a sense of ethics. Even though our work is not regulated, recordkeepers, like historians, journalists, and statisticians, adhere to ethical frameworks that help guide our actions. I think we should also apply ethical standards to the development of information technology. Data protection and privacy commissioners from around the world have taken an important step in this regard, approving a *Declaration on Ethics and Data Protection in Artificial Intelligence* at their October 2018 conference. This declaration states that the "creation, development and use of artificial intelligence systems shall fully respect human rights, particularly the rights to the protection of personal data and to privacy, as well as human dignity, non-discrimination and fundamental values."[13] Demanding respect for human rights in the development of potentially intrusive information technologies should not be a matter of debate.

Partnerships and alliances are also important. Recordkeeping professionals actively seek out champions in the public sector: writers, historians, journalists, or lawyers who will advocate on behalf of evidence, accountability, and good governance. But a recordkeeper's voice is weak compared with the voice of a concerned public. In addition to arguing for strong and effective recordkeeping laws, Canadian archivist Richard Valpy has made a compelling case for the establishment of what he calls a Canadian Documentary Heritage Commission, made up of leading figures across the nation who can bring public attention to problems related to the protection and management of evidence. The efforts of a group of concerned citizens would be much more effective in raising awareness of the importance of effective evidence management than those of a small and under-recognized group of professionals. The recordkeeping profession, dedicated as we are, cannot make enough noise by ourselves.[14]

How much change would happen if one celebrity or influencer took up the cause of evidence management? What if historians like Ken Burns or Mary Beard or organizations like the American Historical Association, the Society of Professional Journalists, or the American Statistical Association spoke out for the protection of evidence? They could have such a powerful impact if they argued not just in support of historical research or journalism but also to uphold accountability and enhance community, memory, identity, and democracy.

To fight the post-truth fake news world, we also need to fight our own biases, which can be so easy to embrace, like a warm bath on a cold day. Can we distinguish accurate evidence from false information, fact from opinion? Do we take the time to read beyond headlines and Twitter highlights? The Internet pushes skewed and slanted information at us every day, based on the computations and calculations of those troublesome algorithms. As writer and entrepreneur Nat Eliason has argued, the Internet is like "the Las Vegas strip, where you're bombarded with demands for your attention and need not exert any effort to be entertained."[15] We need to resist such a passive approach, especially when democracy is on the line. We should reject superficial and scanty historical analyses, shoddy statistics, and political spin. When we hear lies, we should call them lies. Not alternative facts. Not fake news. Lies.

We should also support the journalists, historians, statisticians, and scientists who access and interpret evidence on our behalf. The average person does not have the luxury, even if that person has the inclination, to wade through the miles and miles of paper and digital evidence that document a news story, history book, or statistical report. We all rely on specialists, who in turn rely on verifiable sources of evidence. If experts were not out there doing the research so that we could read the results, I fear that journalism, history, and science would deteriorate. And as fewer people made use of sources of evidence, a disinterested corporation could say, "No one seems to be using our records or archives. Why should we bother to preserve them?" A municipal government could stop supporting open government if no one demanded evidence of its decisions. A state government could let its recordkeeping processes lapse if it did not have to abide by regulations requiring it to respond to requests within a reasonable time.

Journalists, historians, and scientists hold power brokers accountable by interpreting evidence. Recordkeepers provide the ammunition—the evidence—so that others can use it to fight against obfuscation and deception. As argued by John Sheridan, Digital Director at the United Kingdom's National Archives, archives are sources of trustworthy evidence, essential tools "in an arms race against the forces of fakery."[16] When newspapers wither, histories go unwritten, and statistical analyses are not prepared, what happens to memory, identity, or democracy? The simple act of subscribing to a newspaper, purchasing a history book, or reading a government report can make an immeasurable difference in the perception public agencies have of the value of evidence.

We also need to teach our children, and the generations to come, to respect not only truth and facts but also evidence and proof. If today's children, who are "born digital," grow up understanding the value of evidence, recordkeepers three decades from now will not have to keep fighting with their corporate bosses for the resources needed to manage records and archives. The bosses will "get it," just as we want corporate bosses to "get" the importance of environmental management today.

It is entirely possible and eminently sensible to teach children to be more discerning about data, information, and evidence. It is happening right now. In June 2018, the BBC reported on a study by academics in Uganda and Norway who worked with 10,000 students in Kampala to assess how well children could learn critical thinking skills. They discovered that children could quickly learn how to recognize deceptive or dubious claims of fact. After a short training period, children as young as 10 were able to distinguish between the scientific basis for viruses like HIV/AIDS and local myths about the disease.[17] Children are sponges. They can learn anything and everything. All we need to do is start teaching them.

The problem is not with the children. It is with us, especially those of us, like me, who self-identify as digital immigrants. Baby boomers and Gen Xers remember a world before smartphones and talking refrigerators. Today's children, who will be the politicians and government leaders of 2030, will never know a world before computers. If they are going to listen to our advice, it had better be good. A study under way by the London School of Economics' Truth, Trust & Technology Commission called "Children's Data and Privacy Online: Growing Up in a Digital Age," which assesses children's perceptions of privacy, has found that when parents are lax in the protection of privacy, their children are also lax. How will we teach our children to value privacy and protect evidence if we do not take those goals seriously ourselves?[18]

Embracing Change

One way to take evidence more seriously is to become much more engaged with it. Archival institutions, libraries, and museums all exist for the public. The materials they hold—archives, publications, and artifacts—are kept for the public. We should all take advantage of these wonderful resources. Too often, though, people today assume that if they can't find something on the Internet, it doesn't exist. As I hope I've illuminated in this book, only the smallest portion of documentary evidence will ever be found online. Vast quantities of paper records will never be digitized. No institution has (or ever will have) the time or money to convert all its holdings. And some evidence, whether analog or digital, should not be made available online anyway. Protecting personal privacy is a core part of the archival remit, and some records simply cannot and should not be "out there" indiscriminately. Rather than abandon our genealogical search because Googling our grandmother's last name gives us no hits, we need to dig deeper. The joy that comes from seeing original family photographs, essential legal documents, or personal diaries is indescribable. The door to the repositories holding those documents is wide open. Walk in. Look around. Spend some time. You'll love it.

Indeed, archivists need and want you, the public, to help us make this irreplaceable documentary evidence available. David Ferriero, Archivist of the United States, is working to cultivate "citizen archivists" by creating opportunities for the public to transcribe, describe, and comment on the records held by NARA. He has also initiated a collaborative program with *Wikipedia* to encourage researchers to add information about archival documents to *Wikipedia* articles, with the goal of increasing public access to NARA's holdings. Just down the road from NARA, the Library of Congress has adopted an "aggressive" digitization program in order to support the widest possible engagement with users. North of the border, Library and Archives Canada runs a crowdsourcing initiative, Co-Lab, that allows the public to transcribe documents, tag records, and describe and contextualize archives, so they can "play a role in the narrative of our history."[19]

Documentary evidence doesn't just live in archival repositories: records and archives are critical components of museums and galleries too. Museums, historical centers, libraries, and other cultural institutions actively integrate archival materials into their exhibits and outreach initiatives. As noted by Robyn van Dyk, Head of the Research Centre at the Australian War Memorial, the goal is to draw on all types of evidence, physical and documentary, to weave together not just a story of war but of Australian society. Seeing the archival materials integrated into displays, van Dyk believes, lets visitors feel they are part of the story.[20]

Just as subscribing to a newspaper can help encourage a local government to protect evidence, the simple act of visiting an archival institution, admiring an exhibit of documents in a museum, or viewing the photographs in a local gallery display can make an immeasurable difference. Governments pay attention to statistics; they look closely at how many people visit an archival facility or engage with a digital resource. News outlets fund investigative, evidence-based journalism by generating some revenue from their products. Municipalities are happy to fund community history projects when they know the community enjoys the results. Universities keep teaching history not only because it is important but also because it is popular. The more people study history, the more support archival institutions will receive. "Use it or lose it" is a very real danger. It is not enough to ensure archives are well made and well stored. We all need to value diverse sources of evidence, use them, and support their protection.

Archival materials are not just "old stuff," lying passively in storage depots. They are exciting and dynamic and ever-changing resources, open to continual interpretation and reinterpretation. Archivists want to break down barriers, real and perceived, between our materials and the public, by making archives available as broadly as possible: in research rooms, museum exhibits, gallery displays, and library collections. Archives are not for the elite. They are for everyone. Look for them. Use them. Enjoy them. They are evidence of us.

Evidence faces a precarious future. In a post-truth age, many people just ignore the evidence. But others see the evidence, realize its importance, and do all they can to eradicate it. We must stop them. We cannot allow people in positions of power to destroy evidence because it does not suit their political ambitions, business interests, or personal preferences. Just as we are coming to realize how important it is to protect our environment, we must recognize the urgent need to protect our evidence. We need to strengthen laws, improve technologies, take personal responsibility for our own evidence, and raise public awareness of its value to society.

It is not "just" data. It is not "just" information. It is evidence. Its existence as trustworthy proof enriches all our lives. Its misuse and loss are tragic and irreversible. We need to change course. But recordkeeping professionals cannot do this alone. We need the public to lobby for new laws, press for the ethical use of technologies, support public awareness of the importance of evidence, and appreciate the value of their own evidence, from family letters to digital photographs. Accountability depends on evidence. Trust depends on evidence. Truth depends on evidence.

NOTES

1. See Geoffrey Vendeville, "U of T Hackathon to Save Climate Data before Trump Presidency Brings 'Overwhelming Reaction,'" *U of T News*, December 29, 2016, https://www.utoronto.ca/news/u-t-hackathon-save-climate-data-trump-presidency-brings-overwhelming-reaction, *archived at* https://perma.cc/Z3LP-CWGE.

2. Various news reports about the manipulation of environmental evidence include Annie Snider, "White House, EPA Headed Off Chemical Pollution Study," *Politico*, May 14, 2018, https://www.politico.com/story/2018/05/14/emails-white-house-interfered-with-science-study-536950, *archived at* https://perma.cc/2U7F-PGRR; Associated Press, "EPA Chief Scott Pruitt Personally Monitored Removal of Climate Info from Website," *CBS News*, February 2, 2018, https://www.cbsnews.com/news/epa-chief-scott-pruitt-personally-monitored-removal-of-climate-info-from-website, *archived at* https://perma.cc/D58E-QRN4; and "Interior Official Suggests Deleting Fishing Data That 'Undercuts' Administration's Position," *The Washington Post*, n.d., https://apps.washingtonpost.com/g/documents/national/interior-official-suggests-deleting-fishing-data-that-undercuts-administrations-position/3112, *archived at* https://

perma.cc/U8FX-NPBN and https://perma.cc/AL6H-H2PX. The *Washington Post* document and other examples are discussed in Michael Greshko, Laura Parker, Brian Clark Howard, Daniel Stone, Alejandra Borunda, and Sarah Gibbens, "A Running List of How President Trump Is Changing Environmental Policy," *National Geographic*, April 11, 2019, https://news.nationalgeographic.com/2017/03/how-trump-is -changing-science-environment/?user.testname=photogallery:3, *archived at* https:// perma.cc/RF8H-73SN.

3. I acknowledge that we have not moved fast enough to address climate change, as demonstrated in the October 2018 report from the United Nations' Intergovernmental Panel on Climate Change, which warned the world to reduce human-caused emissions of carbon dioxide (CO2) dramatically in order to halt climate change. (See the IPCC press release and report at https://www.ipcc.ch/news_and_events/ pr_181008_P48_spm.shtml, *archived at* https://perma.cc/VA6P-RY62.) But weaknesses in our efforts at environmental protection do not give us a pass when it comes to protecting evidence.

4. An analysis of the impact of pollution control was published by the Oxford Martin Programme on Global Development at the University of Oxford; see Hannah Ritchie and Max Roser, "Air Pollution," OurWorldInData.org, last revised October 2017, https://ourworldindata.org/air-pollution, *archived at* https://perma.cc/ EYX6-69Z6.

5. In 2016, Canada's information and privacy commissioners called on their respective governments to legislate a "duty to document," requiring public agencies to document "matters related to their deliberations, actions and decisions." The commissioners also urged stronger oversight and enforcement of government recordkeeping, to ensure Canadians would have ongoing and effective access to public records. This recommendation has not yet come to pass. The text of the communication from Canada's federal, provincial, and territorial information commissioners to the Government of Canada can be accessed online through the website of the Office of the Information Commissioner of Canada at www.oic-ci .gc.ca/eng/resolution-obligation-de-documenter_resolution-duty-to-document.aspx, *archived at* https://perma.cc/J7L6-2QSG. In Australia, the government's information management standard offers a promising model for efficiency, effectiveness, and accountability. The standard is constructed on eight key principles that help any government or organization "make and keep good records," including requirements that evidence necessary for government business be systematically governed, created as a matter of course, adequately described, suitably stored in systems that are well managed and maintained, preserved for as long as needed, destroyed or transferred appropriately, and always available for use or reuse until such time as it is no longer needed. For more on the Australian information standard and the work of the National Archives of Australia to establish accountable recordkeeping systems, see the information on the NAA website at www.naa .gov.au/information-management/information-management-standard/index.aspx, *archived at* https://perma.cc/EGD8-QH8Z.

6. Michael Schudson, *The Rise of the Right to Know: Politics and the Culture of Transparency, 1945–1975* (Cambridge, MA: Belknap Press, 2015), 260.

7. Quoted in Lauren Aratani, "Altered Video of CNN Reporter Jim Acosta Heralds a Future Filled with 'Deep Fakes,'" *Forbes*, November 8, 2018, https://www.forbes .com/sites/laurenaratani/2018/11/08/altered-video-of-cnn-reporter-jim-acosta -heralds-a-future-filled-with-deep-fakes/#5b1d2edc3f6c, *archived at* https://perma .cc/JP2A-V4CY.

8. See, for example, the list offered by SplashData, a company that provides password security systems, "100 Worst Passwords of 2017! The Full List," https://www.teams id.com/worst-passwords-2017-full-list, *archived at* https://perma.cc/XJ8L-7P98.

9. See Daisuke Wakabayashi, "Google Plus Will Be Shut Down After User Information Was Exposed," *The New York Times*, October 18, 2018, https://www.nytimes.com/ 2018/10/08/technology/google-plus-security-disclosure.html, *archived at* https:// perma.cc/K47N-ZHLA.

10. John Herrman, "It's Almost 2019. Do You Know Where Your Photos Are?" *The New York Times*, November 29, 2018, https://www.nytimes.com/2018/11/29/style/ digital-photo-storage-purge.html, *archived at* https://perma.cc/PUN8-ESWF.

11. Ken Burns, "Prepared Text of the 2016 Stanford Commencement Address by Ken Burns" (Stanford University, June 12, 2016), https://news.stanford.edu/2016/ 06/12/prepared-text-2016-stanford-commencement-address-ken-burns, *archived at* https://perma.cc/2GWA-CTWM.

12. The official website for the March for Science is at https://www.marchforscience .com, *archived at* https://perma.cc/7PMJ-V3NL.

13. The declaration as adopted at the 2018 International Conference of Data Protection and Privacy Commissioners, on October 23, 2018, is available at https://icdppc.org/ wp-content/uploads/2018/10/20180922_ICDPPC-40th_AI-Declaration_ADOPTED .pdf, *archived at* https://perma.cc/9JLK-HS7X.

14. D. Richard Valpy, "From Missionaries to Managers: Making the Case for a Canadian Documentary Heritage Commission," *Archivaria* 82 (Fall 2016): 137–63.

15. Nat Eliason, "The Destructive Switch from Search to Social," NatEliason.com blog, "Social," n.d., https://www.nateliason.com/blog/search-to-social, *archived at* https://perma.cc/T7G5-9MJB.

16. To hear John Sheridan discuss the importance of protecting digital evidence in the information age, listen to the podcast interview with fellow recordkeeping professional Cassie Findlay, "Recordkeeping Roundcasts, Episode 1: Scale and Complexity with John Sheridan," Recordkeeping Roundtable, August 1, 2018, https://rkroundtable.org/2018/08/01/recordkeeping-roundcasts-episode-1 -scale-and-complexity-with-john-sheridan, *archived at* https://perma.cc/58QP -V7TQ.

17. The study was discussed in the BBC podcast "You Can Handle the Truth," *The Documentary*, June 13, 2018, https://www.bbc.co.uk/programmes/w3csxgn3, *archived at* https://perma.cc/V4XN-J228.

18. See Sonia Livingstone, "Children: A Special Case for Privacy?" *Intermedia* 46, no. 2 (2018): 19. For more on the Children's Data and Privacy Online project, see www .lse.ac.uk/media-and-communications/research/research-projects/childprivacy online, *archived at* https://perma.cc/D7B6-H69H. See also the project blog at http://blogs.lse.ac.uk/parenting4digitalfuture/2018/09/06/theorising-privacy -how-do-and-how-should-children-know, *archived at* https://perma.cc/XP3U-EZH8.

19. See David Ferriero's blog at https://aotus.blogs.archives.gov/about-the-archivist, *archived at* https://perma.cc/MG7B-XQTJ, and the Citizen Archivist Dashboard at https://www.archives.gov/citizen-archivist, *archived at* https://perma.cc/7P4Z -PGAS. The Library of Congress's five-year strategic plan for 2019–2023 is available at https://www.loc.gov/portals/static/strategic-plan/documents/LOC_Strat_Plan _2018.pdf, *archived at* https://perma.cc/Q2TJ-MVXN. For more on LAC's Co-Lab, see the website at https://co-lab.bac-lac.gc.ca/eng, *archived at* https://perma.cc/ 9LBA-H53N. See also the press release "Library and Archives Canada Launches Co-Lab," *Markets Insider*, April 18, 2018, https://markets.businessinsider.com/ news/stocks/library-and-archives-canada-launches-co-lab-1021502754, *archived at* https://perma.cc/LP4L-QXVL.

20. Meeting with Robyn van Dyk, Head, Research Centre, Australian War Memorial, December 6, 2018.

Conclusion

Truth isn't truth.
Rudy Giuliani, 2018

IN AN APPEARANCE ON NBC'S SUNDAY MORNING PUBLIC AFFAIRS
program *Meet the Press*, on August 19, 2018, Donald Trump's personal lawyer,
Rudy Giuliani, got into an argument with the program's host, journalist Chuck
Todd. Giuliani was trying to justify why the White House was taking so long to
grant an interview between the president and Robert Mueller during Mueller's
probe into Russian interference in the 2016 presidential election—an investigation that takes us back into the vortex that surrounds the use and misuse of
evidence.[1]

Getting agitated, Giuliani battled with Todd, saying, "When you tell me
[Trump] should testify because he's going to tell the truth so he shouldn't
worry, well that's so silly because it's somebody's version of the truth, not the
truth." When Todd pressed him, Giuliani came back with this startling response:
"Truth isn't truth."[2]

What?

The problem with Giuliani's controversial statement is that, in many ways,
it is true. (If saying so doesn't take us down another vortex entirely.) Personal truths are true to the person who believes them. They may be false and
irrelevant to everyone else. My declaration that purple is my favorite color is
a personal truth. My husband's preference for Janis Joplin over Queen is his
personal truth. (Go figure.) It is a scientific truth that granite is hard. It is a
personal truth that granite is pretty. It is a medical truth that stubbing a toe
causes physical pain. Believing, as your screaming four-year-old does, that it is
the worst pain in the world is her personal truth. (One that will be refuted by
facts five minutes later, when she is running through the playground and about

to clunk her head on the swing set. Which will result in the next worst pain in the world.)

When a person testifies, whether before a judge or a special counsel, that person—that witness—is supposed to tell the truth, the whole truth, and nothing but the truth. But we cannot see into the witness's brain. We don't know that person's truth. We can rely on nothing but the strength of the witness's personal memories, coupled with that person's sense of integrity. But we all know how fallible our memories can be. And much as we would hope otherwise, not everyone wakes up in the morning driven by the quest to be the most scrupulously honest person on the planet. We need other sources of proof. We need evidence. Truth isn't truth. But proof is proof.

The ICO investigation into Facebook and Cambridge Analytica gave us proof, in the form of a final report and accompanying source evidence gathered during the research and analysis. More than 40 ICO investigators contacted 172 organizations, of which 30 were investigated further. Investigators communicated with nearly 100 individuals and reviewed 700 terabytes of digital data, equivalent to 52.5 billion pages of evidence. The abundance of easily accessible evidence to support the Cambridge Analytica/Facebook case was remarkable. As the Information Commissioner noted, "It is exceptional in that many of the key players have offered their evidence publicly in various parliamentary and media forums around the world, and at different times."[3]

Proof was certainly not so easy to come by during the special counsel's investigation into Russian interference. As Mueller noted, "The investigation did not always yield admissible information or testimony, or a complete picture of the activities undertaken by subjects of the investigation." Some individuals, Mueller noted, invoked their Fifth Amendment right not to incriminate themselves. Other sources of evidence were restricted by legal privilege. Some individuals provided false or incomplete information. Others, including some directly associated with Donald Trump's presidential campaign, "deleted relevant communications or communicated during the relevant period using applications that feature encryption or that do not provide for long-term retention of data or communications records."[4] As a result, Mueller concluded that

> while this report embodies factual and legal determinations that the Office believes to be accurate and complete to the greatest extent possible, given these identified gaps, the Office cannot rule out the possibility that the unavailable information would shed additional light on (or cast in a new light) the events described in the report.[5]

In the end, Mueller confirmed that a foreign government *did* interfere in the 2016 presidential election. He also determined that there was not enough evidence to lay criminal charges of American conspiracy in that interference. He concluded that there was insufficient evidence to prove, again for the purposes of criminal charges, that the president or his associates obstructed justice. But as Mueller wrote, the absence of conclusive evidence does not exonerate. New evidence would lead to new conclusions, new truths.[6]

The legal analysis of the Mueller report is beyond me. Like philosophy, the law is well above my pay grade. What is clear to me, though, in my capacity as a recordkeeping expert, is this: In the normal execution of government affairs, a great deal of evidence that would have emerged during an investigation like this ought to have been created and kept as a matter of course. In this instance, much of that evidence is missing. Was it misplaced? Lost? Destroyed? Never created in the first place? I do not believe those responsible for such lapses ought to get a pass because the evidence needed to prove their wrongdoing is now gone. The law is a hard taskmaster, and the burden of proof for criminal charges is high. But from a recordkeeper's perspective, the absence of evidence is evidence. Those responsible for its loss should be held to account.

Evidence is not a frill. It is a cornerstone of an accountable, responsible democracy. We need to shed the assumption that evidence—records, archives, and verifiable data—will be created as naturally as breathing and then will continue to exist, authentic, whole, and intact, for as long as we want. We used to wait for evidence to get old before it was taken into custody and preserved for some future historian to use. In the age of instant information, we need to preserve digital evidence now, before it is altered, lost, or destroyed.

Evidence is under attack. Information and records are weapons now. Emails are deleted so we cannot prove people's actions or decisions. Paper documents are ripped up and digital copies wiped from hard drives. Video recordings are manipulated to show people doing things they did not do. Photographs can be altered to remove or add people seamlessly. Reports can be rewritten after the fact, with no way to see the changes. Voices on audio recordings are faked, giving new meaning to the expression "Don't put words in my mouth."

When the film *Forrest Gump* came out in 1994, a lot of archivists, including me, were incensed with the reckless manipulation of evidence. Director Robert Zemeckis had inserted images of Tom Hanks into archival footage, showing his character, Forrest Gump, participating in a series of actual historical events. He met President Kennedy; he received a Medal of Honor from President Johnson; he stayed at the Watergate Hotel the night of the burglary that brought down President Nixon. My recordkeeping friends and I condemned this blending of reality and falsehood, which we thought made a mockery of truth and proof. Archivists might not have laughed, but the public loved the film. They could see the deception, I guess, and they knew it was a joke. Now we can't see the deception, and it is no joke.[7]

At a White House press conference on November 7, 2018, following the US midterm elections, Donald Trump criticized CNN journalist Jim Acosta, calling him a "rude, terrible person," a reporter of "fake news," and an "enemy of the people." When a White House aide removed the microphone from Acosta's hand, the exchange was documented in several different video recordings. The White House later revoked Acosta's press pass, claiming he had placed his hands on the aide in an inappropriate manner. The White House produced a video recording as evidence. Several technical specialists who reviewed that footage argued that it had been manipulated: it had been edited to speed up some sections while slowing others, making it look like Acosta had hit the aide with a "karate chop" motion. Even Kellyanne Conway entangled herself in her own defense of the White House video, agreeing that it had been sped up but denying that it had been edited.[8]

On October 2, 2018, the journalist Jamal Khashoggi was murdered after he entered the Saudi Arabian consulate in Istanbul, Turkey, to obtain paperwork needed to marry his Turkish fiancée, Hatice Cengiz. Khashoggi, who had a long career as a journalist and an editor, most recently writing for *The Washington Post*, had been critical of Saudi Arabia's crown prince, Mohammad bin Salman, and had opposed many Saudi actions, including the country's significant role in the war in Yemen.[9]

After Khashoggi entered the consulate, he disappeared. CCTV video evidence showed Khashoggi walking into the building, but no comparable evidence existed to show that he ever left. Until another video emerged, showing "him" leaving the consulate by a back entrance. It turned out this video was fake; the person shown was an impersonator, wearing clothes just like Khashoggi's. Then audio evidence appeared that seemed to recount the actual killing. Traced phone calls revealed conversations between members of the alleged hit team confirming the murder. Which sources of evidence are real? Which are false? Solving a murder depends on trustworthy evidence, not on gut instincts and personal truths.[10]

It is no coincidence that George Orwell has become such a literary touchstone today. His dystopian novel *Nineteen Eighty-Four*, published just after the end of World War II, depicted the lies and deceit he saw as an integral part of the Cold War unfolding before him. Today, there is a teachable moment on just about every page of that novel. One passage is particularly appropriate for my purposes:

And when memory failed and written records were falsified—when that happened, the claim of the Party to have improved the conditions of human life had got to be accepted, because there did not exist, and never again could exist, any standard against which it could be tested.[11]

In Orwell's book, Winston Smith was a government archivist. But far from being a keeper of evidence, he was, in this upside-down world, a manipulator of facts. He falsified documents as part of his responsibility to protect "truth." One day, though, he decided to defy the power brokers at the Ministry of Truth. He started keeping a personal diary and (perhaps more egregiously) he fell in love. He was tortured into betraying his lover (who also betrayed him), and he was tormented into declaring falsehoods as fact. Even though he was lying, and there was proof to show he was lying, Winston ended up declaring that, yes, Oceania was at war with Eastasia. That Oceania had always been at war with Eastasia. That two and two made five. Every statement he declared as truth was a lie. Not a glass-half-full/glass-half-empty alternative fact. A lie. If the evidence keeper cannot find the truth, dystopia is real.

The recordkeeper's job is to support truth. Not personal truths, or partial truths, or relative truths, but evidence-based truths. As much as anyone can be, recordkeepers—whether we are called archivists or records managers or information analysts or whatever—strive to be impartial and objective. We work on behalf of society, today and for the future. As David Ferriero, Archivist of the United States, has argued so eloquently,

> The importance of independent archives at all levels of government is critical to the trust of the country in its history, and the ability of the archives to provide reliable trustworthy evidence of the actions of the past. Every government archivist must be allowed to do his or her job free of political pressure so that the archival record can speak freely, and so the archives can continue to function as the trusted repository of the actions of government.[12]

If archivists cannot capture and protect the sources of proof, if we cannot ensure they are authentic and trustworthy and reliable, if those sources are lost before we even get to them, or if we are allowed only the evidence that suits a particular perspective, then all of society will suffer. We must fight back.

Unlike Winston Smith, Star Trek's Captain Jean-Luc Picard fought back. On Star Date 2369, some 385 years after Smith's shameful disgrace, Picard was tortured by the brutal Cardassian interrogator Gul Madred. Madred told Picard he would be released if he agreed to do one small thing. All he had to do was confirm that he saw five lights on the ceiling, not four. (Two and two make five redux.) But Captain Picard was able to hold on to his own truth. A protector of facts, fighting against political pressure regardless of the torture he faced, Picard clung to his belief in the evidence, repeatedly and fervently shouting that "there are *four* lights."[13]

Holding on to truth is perhaps the greatest challenge we face in this post-truth world. We must all fight back against lies, false facts, and the manipulation of evidence. As the political commentator David Frum argues, in his perceptive analysis of the dystopian world that is Donald Trump's presidency, we need to remember, and protect, the "preciousness of truth." "If there is no truth," Frum argues, "there can be no lying."[14]

We must—*we must*—actively disavow lies, challenge falsehoods, and reject the distortion or abuse of evidence. If we see four lights, if we know for a fact that there are four lights, if we have proof of those four lights, then we must declare this evidence-based truth. And we must preserve the evidence of those four lights, to counter lies and deceit with facts. Provable facts.

When I began my career as an archivist, my job was to manage the "old" archives that had survived flood and fire and office purges, to make the precious slivers of documentary gold available for scholars and genealogists, government officials, and family historians. Everyone trusted that what was new would naturally become old, and that there was a logical path from office to repository. The path was bumpy, sure, but the people at the receiving end—my end—had little or no say in how to smooth it out. We managed what came to us. We may have wanted to be in at the beginning, but that was not how it was done.

When power was in the hands of so few—kings and popes and generals—the public rarely saw the proof, not for centuries after the fact. Now we have dash cam video of car chases. Police officers wear cameras strapped to their chests. GPS systems track us from home to office to airport. Children can manipulate information on digital tablets by the age of two. We create evidence as naturally as breathing: taking thousands of photographs, sending text messages every hour, posting or tweeting daily on social media. We are surrounded by technologies that help us (or hinder us) as we create quintillions of bytes of data every day, week, and year. We need to grasp the nettle of this evidence problem. We need to work together to come up with solutions, so that the evidence we value so much is protected for today and for the future. The recordkeeper cannot do the job alone. Not in a digital age.

I have a vision. Call it naïve or idealistic, but it is the vision that drives my work as a recordkeeping professional. I want to live in a society that is enlightened, civilized, democratic, respectful, and self-aware. In order to achieve such a society, one that is free, democratic, respectful, and self-aware, people need a recorded memory. They need to be able to create a collective consciousness from unfettered access to the evidence of communications, actions, and transactions. Open and easy access to sources of trustworthy evidence helps to support democracy, transparency, and accountability and to foster a sense of personal and collective identity.

Access to evidence, be it photographs taken yesterday, government records produced last month, or diaries written a century ago, helps people know themselves and their world, offering tangible proof of their lives and work. Documentary evidence, along with books and films and stories and movies and songs and art, help people and societies understand and value themselves and each other, fostering identity and memory. These diverse sources of evidence also help people remember and understand—themselves and each other; good and bad—generating pride, humility, and honest reflection by reminding them of the efforts and experiences of their predecessors, from distant ancestors to contemporary acquaintances.

I want to live in a society where people see the value in evidence and respect and appreciate the people documented in that evidence. We can work together to create this society. Archivists cannot do it alone anymore. We *all* need to come together to preserve the documentary evidence that holds to account those in power, that nurtures our sense of identity and community, and that helps us capture and share our individual and collective memories. We need to come together to change course, before it is too late. We are all archivists now.

NOTES

1. Among the many news reports of this exchange is the UK-based *Guardian* report by Ed Pilkington, "'Truth Isn't Truth': Giuliani Trumps 'Alternative Facts' with New Orwellian Outburst," *The Guardian*, August 19, 2018, https://www.theguardian.com/us-news/2018/aug/19/truth-isnt-truth-rudy-giuliani-trump-alternative-facts-orwellian, *archived at* https://perma.cc/XF37-ZLSG.

2. Ibid.

3. Information Commissioner's Office, *Investigation into the Use of Data Analytics in Political Campaigns: A Report to Parliament* (ICO, November 6, 2018), 13–15,

https://ico.org.uk/media/action-weve-taken/2260271/investigation-into-the-use
-of-data-analytics-in-political-campaigns-final-20181105.pdf, *archived at* https://
perma.cc/5GVS-7HYC.

4. Special Counsel Robert S. Mueller, *Report on the Investigation into Russian Interference in the 2016 Presidential Election* (Washington, DC: US Department of Justice,
March 2019), vol. I, p. 10, https://www.justice.gov/sco, *archived at* https://perma
.cc/LQY3-MPVG, as published by *The New York Times*, at https://www.nytimes.com/
interactive/2019/04/18/us/politics/mueller-report-document.html, *archived at*
https://perma.cc/GHN7-2AYF.

5. Ibid.

6. Donald Trump was not interviewed by Mueller, instead answering written questions. According to *The Washington Post*, Trump responded to the questions with
"I don't recall" more than 30 times. A president is a busy person, certainly, and he
or she cannot be expected to recall everything that happens in a day. But that is
why presidents have armies of attendants. To take notes. And to keep those notes.
As required by law. See Philip Bump, "Trump's Most Frequent Contribution to the
Mueller Probe? 'I Don't Recall,'" *The Washington Post*, April 18, 2019, https://www
.washingtonpost.com/politics/2019/04/18/trumps-most-frequent-contribution
-mueller-probe-i-dont-recall/?utm_term=.2ba640be4aaf, *archived at* https://perma
.cc/T2EG-R5KA. As I completed this book in April 2019, scrutiny of the Mueller
report had only just begun. One of the most informative and thoughtful sources
of analysis is *Lawfare*, a blog (and associated essays and podcasts) published by
the Lawfare Institute, in cooperation with the Brookings Institution, which was
founded in 2010 by journalist Benjamin Wittes, formerly of *The Washington Post*,
along with law professors Jack Goldsmith, of the Harvard Law School, and Robert
Chesney, of the University of Texas at Austin. See the *Lawfare* website at https://
www.lawfareblog.com, *archived at* https://perma.cc/4Y3D-NRLE. Among the first
summaries produced by *Lawfare* is Scott R. Anderson, Victoria Clark, Mikhaila
Fogel, Sarah Grant, Susan Hennessey, Matthew Kahn, Quinta Jurecic, Lev Sugar-
man, Margaret Taylor, and Benjamin Wittes, "What Mueller Found on Russia and
on Obstruction: A First Analysis," *Lawfare*, April 18, 2019, https://www.lawfare
blog.com/what-mueller-found-russia-and-obstruction-first-analysis, *archived at*
https://perma.cc/C9RN-LSBW.

7. Apparently, one of the most complicated scenes to create in *Forrest Gump* showed
hundreds of thousands of antiwar protestors on the National Mall in Washington,
DC. In order to show such a huge crowd with only 1,500 extras at his disposal,
Zemeckis arranged for the extras to move from place to place as the scene was
filmed over and over again from different angles. Computer technologies were then
used to replicate the people from different perspectives, resulting in a massive
crowd scene. The story of Zemeckis and the filming of the scene at the National
Mall is found in various sources, including the DVD production *Seeing Is Believing:
The Visual Effects of Forrest Gump—Enhancing Reality* (Los Angeles: Paramount
Pictures, 2001). My question is, was it the largest peace rally ever?

8. Lauren Aratani, "Altered Video of CNN Reporter Jim Acosta Heralds a Future Filled
with 'Deep Fakes,'" *Forbes*, November 8, 2018, https://www.forbes.com/sites/

laurenaratani/2018/11/08/altered-video-of-cnn-reporter-jim-acosta-heralds-a
-future-filled-with-deep-fakes/#5b1d2edc3f6c, *archived at* https://perma.cc/
JP2A-V4CY. The plethora of news stories on this event is overwhelming. See, for
instance, Didi Martinez, "Kellyanne Conway Says Jim Acosta Video Was 'Sped Up,'
but Not 'Doctored,'" *NBC News*, November 12, 2018, https://www.nbcnews.com/
news/all/kellyanne-conway-says-jim-acosta-video-was-sped-not-doctored-n935196,
archived at https://perma.cc/X9TZ-2MQZ.

9. According to the American-based Committee to Protect Journalists, 34 journalists
were murdered around the world in 2018, including Khashoggi. See the CPJ's database and analysis at https://cpj.org, *archived at* https://perma.cc/3VXL-J8K3.

10. Among the many news stories about the killing of Jamal Khashoggi, see Shane
Harris, Greg Miller, and Josh Dawsey, "CIA Concludes Saudi Crown Prince Ordered
Jamal Khashoggi's Assassination," *The Washington Post*, November 16, 2018,
https://www.washingtonpost.com/world/national-security/cia-concludes-saudi
-crown-prince-ordered-jamal-khashoggis-assassination/2018/11/16/98c89fe6
-e9b2-11e8-a939-9469f1166f9d_story.html?noredirect=on&utm_term=.d833
44a205eb, *archived at* https://perma.cc/696X-652Q. See also Gul Tuysuz, Salma
Abdelaziz, Ghazi Balkiz, Ingrid Formanek, and Clarissa Ward, "Surveillance Footage Shows Saudi 'Body Double' in Khashoggi's Clothes after He Was Killed, Turkish
Source Says," *CNN World*, October 23, 2018, https://edition.cnn.com/2018/10/22/
middleeast/saudi-operative-jamal-khashoggi-clothes/index.html, *archived at*
https://perma.cc/MA9Q-JYJF; and Orhan Coskun, "Exclusive: Turkish Police
Believe Saudi Journalist Khashoggi Was Killed in Consulate—Sources," *Reuters
World News*, October 6, 2018, https://www.reuters.com/article/us-saudi-politics
-dissident/exclusive-turkish-police-believe-saudi-journalist-khashoggi-was-killed
-in-consulate-sources-idUSKCN1MG0HU?il=0&utm_source=reddit.com, *archived
at* https://perma.cc/FG9Z-44JB.

11. George Orwell, *Nineteen Eighty-Four* (1949; repr., London: Penguin Classics, 2000),
97.

12. See David Ferriero, "AOTUS David Ferriero's Archives Month Post: Celebrating
American Archives Month," CoSA (Council of State Archivists) blog, October 25,
2018, originally posted October 5, 2018, https://www.statearchivists.org/connect/
blog/2018/10/aotus-david-ferrieros-archives-month-post, *archived at* https://
perma.cc/NW2L-LVDZ.

13. The two-part episode "Chain of Command," from the series *Star Trek: The Next
Generation*, first aired in 1992; see https://www.imdb.com/titlett0708686/?ref
_=tt_ep_pr, *archived at* https://perma.cc/MD55-PHJM. And, by the way, some
people do actually calculate Star Date to Real Date equivalencies; see Andreas
Schmidt, "Calculate the Stardate of the Star Trek Future!," last changed September
16, 2004, http://www.hillschmidt.de/gbr/sternenzeit.htm, *archived at* https://
perma.cc/7PTU-LTBZ.

14. David Frum, *Trumpocracy: The Corruption of the American Public* (New York:
HarperCollins, 2018), 221, 223.

Additional Reading

IN ADDITION TO THE PUBLICATIONS CITED THROUGHOUT THE BOOK, the following selected titles offer insights into such diverse topics as postmodernism, concepts of truth, the nature of evidence, and the impact of digital technologies.

Andersen, Ken. *Fantasyland: How America Went Haywire—A 500 Year His-* 17.

ts: *Why Everything We Know Has an* Current, 2013.

tter Off Forgetting? Essays on Memory. Toronto: University of

ter Challenge to Human Intelligence.

Vires between Americans and Our y, 2017.

ngblood Henderson. *Protecting Global Challenge.* Saskatoon:

est to Regain Public Trust. Toronto:

Benford, Gregory. *Deep Time: How Humanity Communicates across Millennia.* New York: Abbenford Associates, 1999.

Bingham, Tom. *The Rule of Law.* London: Penguin, 2011.

Blouin, Francis X., Jr., and William G. Rosenberg. *Archives, Documentation and Institutions of Social Memory: Essays from the Sawyer Seminar.* Ann Arbor: University of Michigan Press, 2006.

Clanchy, Michael. *From Memory to Written Record: England 1066–1307.* 3rd ed. Chichester, UK: Wiley-Blackwell, 2012.

D'Ancona, Matthew. *Post Truth: The New War on Truth and How to Fight Back.* London: Ebury Press, 2017.

Evans, Richard J. *In Defence of History.* London: Granta, 2018.

Frum, David. *Trumpocracy: The Corruption of the American Republic.* New York: HarperCollins, 2018.

Hedges, Chris. *Empire of Illusion: The End of Literacy and the Triumph of Spectacle.* Toronto: Vintage Canada, 2009.

Kahneman, Daniel. *Thinking Fast and Slow.* London: Penguin, 2011.

Kakutani, Michiko. *The Death of Truth: Notes on Falsehood in the Age of Trump.* New York: Tim Duggan Books, 2018.

Keanneally, Christine. *The Invisible History of the Human Race.* New York: Penguin, 2014.

Klosterman, Chuck. *But What If We're Wrong? Thinking about the Present As If It Were the Past.* New York: Blue Rider Press, 2016.

Macdonald, Hector. *Truth: How the Many Sides to Every Story Shape Our Reality.* Toronto: McClelland & Stewart, 2018.

MacMillan, Margaret. *The Uses and Abuses of History.* Toronto: Viking Canada, 2008.

McIntyre, Lee. *Post-Truth.* Cambridge, MA: MIT Press, 2018.

Morozov, Evgeny, *To Save Everything, Click Here: The Folly of Technological Solutionism.* New York: Public Affairs, 2013.

Newsom, Gavin, with Lisa Dickey. *Citizenville: How to Take the Town Square Digital and Reinvent Government.* New York: Penguin, 2013.

Nichols, Tom. *The Death of Expertise: The Campaign against Established Knowledge and Why It Matters.* Oxford: Oxford University Press, 2017.

O'Neil, Cathy. *Weapons of Math Destruction: How Big Data Increases Inequality and Threatens Democracy.* London: Penguin, 2016.

Owen, Taylor. *Disruptive Power: The Crisis of the State in the Digital Age.* Oxford: Oxford University Press, 2015.

Postman, Neil. *Technopoly: The Surrender of Culture to Technology.* New York: Vintage, 1993.

Schmidt, Eric, and Jared Cohen. *The New Digital Age: Reshaping the Future of People, Nations and Business.* London: John Murray, 2014.

Schudson, Michael. *The Rise of the Right to Know: Politics and the Culture of Transparency, 1945–1975.* Cambridge, MA: Belknap Press, 2015.

Stephens-Davidowitz, Seth. *Everybody Lies: Big Data, New Data, and What the Internet Can Tell Us about Who We Really Are.* New York: HarperCollins, 2018.

Taplin, Jonathan. *Move Fast and Break Things: How Facebook, Google and Amazon Have Cornered Culture and Undermined Democracy.* London: Pan Books, 2018.

Thomas, David, Simon Fowler, and Valerie Johnson. *The Silence of the Archive.* London: Facet, 2017.

Yeo, Geoffrey. *Records, Information, and Data: Exploring the Role of Record-Keeping in an Information Culture.* London: Facet, 2018.

Young, Nora. *The Virtual Self: How Our Digital Lives Are Altering the World Around Us.* Toronto: McClelland & Stewart, 2012.

For More Advice

WOULD YOU LIKE TO KNOW MORE ABOUT WHAT RECORDKEEPING
professionals do? Would you like advice on how to manage your own sources
of evidence or how to get involved with the profession? Feel free to contact an
archivist. We are there for you.

American Library Association
50 East Huron Street
Chicago, Illinois 60611-2795
USA

Tel 312/944-6780
Fax 312/440-9374
Toll-free 800/545-2433
Email: ala@ala.org

Society of American Archivists
17 North State Street, Suite 1425
Chicago, Illinois 60602-4061
USA

Tel 312/606-0722
Fax 312/606-0728
Toll-free 866/722-7858
Email: saahq@archivists.org

Acknowledgments

I AM GRATEFUL TO EVERYONE WHO SUPPORTED MY WORK ON THIS book, from the archivists who shared their expertise and opinions with me to the friends and colleagues who answered my innumerable questions about "What does evidence mean to you?" I am honored that University College London appointed me an Honorary Senior Research Associate, a position that has enhanced my ability to carry out research. My thanks to Chris Prom, Chair of the Society of American Archivists' Publications Board, for his unfailing enthusiasm for the idea of the book, for reviewing outlines and chapters, and for coordinating reviews from members of the board, including Bethany Anderson, Mary Caldera, Sarah Demb, and Amy Cooper Cary. Their feedback on early drafts was very helpful. My thanks also to Rachel Chance, Acquisitions Editor at the American Library Association, for her wise counsel during the development of this book and to Amy Knauer for her meticulous copyediting.

In Canada, Guy Berthiaume, Librarian and Archivist of Canada, graciously welcomed my research inquiries, answering all my questions with enthusiasm and wisdom. He says he is retiring in 2019—he will be missed. The staff at Library and Archives Canada welcomed me unreservedly during my site visit to the institution in June 2018 and responded to all my subsequent queries without hesitation. Special thanks go to LAC representatives Sara Chatfield, Alexandria Clemence, Catherine Bailey, Melanie Brown, Jana Buhlman, Sophie Dazé, Karine Gélinas, Tina Harvey, Danny Krkic, Faye Lemay, Alexandra McEwen, Robert McIntosh, Dino Roberge, Johanna Smith, and Lisa Tremblay-Goodyer.

In Australia, my thanks to David Fricker, Director General of the National Archives of Australia and President of the International Council on Archives, for his insights on the topics addressed in my book and for opening the doors of his institution so I could meet with archival staff to discuss my ideas. Special thanks to Kylie Roth and Monique Nielsen for their kind support. I also appreciate the financial support provided by the National Archives of Australia, which facilitated my travel to Australia to participate in UNESCO Memory of the World meetings in December 2018. Special thanks to Adrian Cunningham for helping to coordinate the visit and for taking time to talk at length about my research. My thanks to staff at the National Library of Australia for welcoming me so warmly, especially to Hilary Berthon, Kevin Bradley, Libor Coufal, Emma Jolley, Cathie Oats, and Mark Piva. I am grateful to Robyn van Dyk at the Australian War Memorial for providing a wealth of information about the role of archives in the creation of stories of Australian identity.

Other archival colleagues provided invaluable input. My sincere appreciation goes to Eiríkur G. Guðmundsson, National Archivist of Iceland; Meg Phillips, External Affairs Liaison, United States National Archives and Records Administration; Anthea Seles, Secretary General of the International Council on Archives; Elizabeth Shepherd, Head of the Department of Information Studies, University College London; and Sarah Tyacke, former Keeper of Public Records for the United Kingdom.

Other friends provided support and suggestions, for which I am very grateful, including Jim Burant, Ann Cowan, Suzanne Dubeau, Michael Dyck, June Harman, Michael Hoyle, Heather MacNeil, John McDonald, Francis Mansbridge, Michael Pasch, Crystal Penner, Barbara Reed, James Shirras, Kelly Stewart, and Geoffrey Yeo. Special thanks to my nephew, software engineer Chris Millar, for his ideas about information technology issues, and to my niece, writer, editor, and journalist Madelaine Millar, who commented on various chapters, offering the perspective of the "born digital" generation.

Richard Valpy read and reread many chapters, as he has done for so many of my writing projects over the years, providing constructive suggestions and unwavering support. Wendy Plain's editorial insights, perceptive analysis, and wise guidance helped transform the manuscript from a collection of ideas to a cohesive whole. I cannot thank her enough for coming to my aid just when I needed help the most.

My husband, Brian Arnold, remains the rock he has been for decades, reading drafts, making tea, cooking meals, and not grumbling when the computer glowed at 3:00 a.m. while I wrestled with the latest wrinkle in the manuscript. Everything good in my life starts with him.

Laura Millar
April 2019

About the Author

DR. LAURA A. MILLAR IS AN INDEPENDENT CONSULTANT AND scholar in records, archives, and information management and has also worked in publishing and distance education. She has consulted with governments, universities, colleges, professional associations, non-profit organizations, and other agencies around the world. Her work has ranged from advising the Government of Hong Kong on best practices in records and archives management to consulting with First Nations' communities in the Canadian arctic on the preservation of indigenous sources of evidence. She was named the winner of the Society of American Archivists' 2011 Waldo Gifford Leland Award for *Archives: Principles and Practices*. She is the author of dozens of publications and conference presentations, and she has taught records and archives management in several universities in Canada and internationally. She lives with her husband in the community of Roberts Creek, on the Sunshine Coast of British Columbia, Canada.

Index